The Ultimate Content Marketing Playbook
For Professional Firms

The Ultimate Content Marketing Playbook
For Professional Firms

Spotlight Branding

Copyright © 2021 by Spotlight Branding

All rights reserved. This book or any portion thereof may not be reproduced or used in any manner whatsoever without the express written permission of the publisher except for the use of brief quotations in a book review or scholarly journal.

First Printing: 2021

Spotlight Branding
9624 Bailey Road, Suite 270
Cornelius, NC 28031

www.spotlightbranding.com

Dedication

For the eternally frustrated business owner who hates marketing because it never seems to work.

Contents

Introduction 1
Chapter 1 ~ The History of Marketing 5
Chapter 2 ~ The Biggest Problem with Modern Marketing 9
Chapter 3 ~ The Answer Is Content 17
Chapter 4 ~ Identifying Your Perfect Client 28
Chapter 5 ~ Your Website: Your Business's First Impression 37
Chapter 6 ~ Blogging: Your Pillar Content Starting Point 48
Chapter 7 ~ Video: The Most Versatile Pillar Content 55
Chapter 8 ~ Podcasting: The Expertise–Boosting Content Medium ...61
Chapter 9 ~ Social Media: Your Community Touchpoint Hub 74
Chapter 10 ~ Email: Your Most Valuable Marketing Asset 80
Chapter 11 ~ Understanding Your Marketing Success 87
Chapter 12 ~ The Obligatory SEO Chapter 92

Introduction

When we published our first book in January 2020, *The Ultimate Solo Lawyer's Guide to More Referrals and Better Clients*, we had no idea how popular it would be. We gave away hundreds of copies to those who requested one, and many more were purchased online. And while nothing in that book has become outdated by any means, we at Spotlight Branding made a full commitment to content marketing and thought it was time to zero in on how truly powerful it can be.

A 2020 Vision Direct poll found that people spend an average of 10 hours a day looking at their computer and smartphone. When most of us aren't working on those devices, we're checking Facebook, scrolling through Instagram, reading emails, catching up on the news, watching videos on YouTube, and more. And what do all of those things have in common? They're all different types of content.

That's where marketing is right now. We are all being fed an abundance information and have a constant stream of products and services placed in front of our eyes on a near continual basis. If your business and products aren't part of that stream, you're falling behind your competition.

The problem is that many lawyers, financial pros, chiropractors, and other small business owners either don't create any content, do it infrequently, or completely ignore the human beings that will be hiring them in favor of appeasing search engine bots and campaigns like billboards or print ads that make it practically impossible to generate some sort of tangible ROI. Regardless of whatever route they take, the destination is always the same—frustration and the belief that marketing doesn't work. However, it's time to rethink that.

Imagine your marketing strategy like a custom built home. It's foolish to build a house on the first plot of land you can find without clearing the area and leveling the surface. In order to build a stable house, you need timber formwork to outline your foundation and concrete to set the plane.

That foundation is your website and your content. It's the central hub that all of your marketing points back to. **If you don't have a website, put this book down and go get one made.** You will not grow your business without a website in place. It's the first impression your business will make and the first place people will look when they want to learn more about you.

The content—blogs, videos, podcasts, social media posts, and emails—gives you a solid and secure foundation to build on. From there, you build upon that foundation with all of your other marketing efforts, whatever you want them to be. And because your house (i.e., your business) was built on a strong foundation, your marketing will provide you with everything you need it to be and more. The house built hastily on uneven ground quickly becomes unstable and unsafe.

If that wonderful analogy didn't convince you that content should be your firm's marketing focus, the rest of this book will aim to finish the job. We'll give you additional context as to why content is so important, how content impacts referrals, and how those specific leads make for the best clients. We'll then talk about how content elevates your expertise before diving deep into the various forms of content available to you so you can create a rock solid marketing foundation for your business.

In the end, this book will provide you with a complete playbook that you can start implementing immediately in your business, complete with specific prompts and ideas that you can run with to turn your business into a content-generating machine.

Why a playbook? We'll admit that we're big football fans around the office, and we think it's such a perfect analogy for how to approach your marketing and business development. Every football team has a playbook that describes every position's duties to keep everyone on the same page. Without it, every play would be chaos.

Your business can have several different playbooks, such as your Policies & Procedures manual, your internal processes, and of course your marketing strategy (which is what this book is here to help you build!). If all of your plays (AKA your policies, strategies, etc.) are written down in detail and put in place, you and your employees know what they need to accomplish.

While we're at it, there are some other things you business can learn from a football team, such as:

1. Developing a strategy

Some teams throw the ball a lot while others rely on a bruising running game. Some teams blitz the opposing quarterback while others drop back in coverage. Neither strategy in a vacuum is better than the other, but having one, building your team around it, and executing it to the fullest brings a team together to accomplish the goal of winning the game.

2. Clearly defining positions

While this book is strictly about marketing, football teams are all about making sure they have the right guys in the right spot on the field. A guy who can't catch won't make for a good wide receiver just like someone who sounds bored or annoyed on the phone won't make a good receptionist. Make sure your business has the right coaches (managers) and players (employees) who not only know their roles inside and out, but can execute them at the highest level. (Be on the lookout for a future book from us covering the lessons we've learned about business development.)

3. Building a brand

Is your business the football equivalent of "America's Team," "The Monsters of the Midway," or "The Greatest Show on Turf"? Just like these infamous teams, those slogans exist to sell the team and hype up the fans. Your clients are your fans and your brand should stand out through the content you produce. Every fan base is different, but you can win yours over by creating a brand, message, and content that appeals directly to them.

We truly appreciate you taking the time to read this book. If you have any questions about the information in this book or you want to talk further about your marketing strategy, we are always available to chat.

Send us an email at Solutions@SpotlightBranding.com or give us a call at (800) 406-7229.

Chapter 1 ~ The History of Marketing

Our content guru, John Hinson, really loves history. He enjoys it so much that he's published 20 books as his own little side hobby, most of which deal with historical topics that don't get talked about a lot (we may have also used that as an excuse to get him to put this book together). Because of his special hobby, he looks at the world through a particular lens and has noticed something strange about the marketing world.

If you look at the marketing landscape today, you'd likely assume that the only marketing that has ever worked is cold lead generation from search engines. (Do we really even remember how the world worked before the internet?) You, as a business owner, have likely received dozens, if not hundreds, of cold sales emails from various vendors offering all kinds of search engine optimization packages and page–one guarantees for just a few hundred dollars per month.

And unless you took marketing classes in college, you'd likely think that was the primary way people market their business these days. Of course that's not true.

That's why John is also a huge fan of context. The more he knows about the circumstances, patterns, and history of a particular concept or issue, the better he can understand the present and plan for the future. With that in mind, he thought it would be helpful to start this book with a helpful dose of context and give you an abbreviated history of branding and marketing to show you that what other "experts" claim is the only thing that works is likely nothing more than just a fad.

While the term "marketing" didn't appear in a dictionary until 1897, the actual practices and actions that we understand as marketing go all the way back to antiquity. Archaeologists have found evidence of branding dating as far back as the 4th century B.C. in Mesopotamia where larger civilizations used stone and clay seals with pressed images to identify their alcoholic drinks, textiles, and other items (that's nearly 2,500 years!). For example, a bottle of Umbricius Scauras fish sauce dating back to 35 B.C. was found in Pompeii. This sauce was well–known throughout most of Europe for its quality in large part due to its unique branding and bottle style—a tall vase with a long, slender neck and a large, thin handle.

Additionally, the Staffelter Hof Winery in Germany has been in operation since 862 AD. How do you think people—including Roman soldiers—would have known about this wine and traveled hundreds of miles to purchase bottles for themselves? By referral!

As time passed and societies progressed, traveling salesmen were joined by markets that housed a collection of vendors selling their branded items. These, of course, soon turned into permanent, individual brick–and–mortar shops selling items that were created by that singular vendor.

So why is all of this important now? Because obviously things like the internet weren't around back then. The printing press and modern newspaper publication didn't come around until the early 1600s, which means the only kind of marketing that existed back then was word of mouth and referrals.

And it worked. It has always worked. And if you think marketing doesn't work, we've just given you 2,500 years' worth of proof that it does.

The point here is that referrals and word of mouth have not only existed for thousands of years, but it has been the most effective way of marketing a business. It just works, plain and simple!

But when the internet rose to prominence in the late 1990s, there was a shift in marketing philosophy. By then, radio and television ads were prominent. There were also ads on billboards and park benches, inside phone books, and through direct mail. And while all of those campaigns got results, nothing ever matched the quality and ease of working with people who found a business through a referral.

Yet over the last 15 years or so, referrals have almost been an afterthought even though there is no data to suggest they aren't as effective as they once were. Businesses today just assume they're going to get referrals and don't consider that they could be getting more (or even better, that the majority of their business can come from referrals).

They also don't consider the fact that (according to a collection of studies by OutboundEngine) it costs five times more money to acquire a new customer than it does to retain an existing one. Additionally, the success rate of selling a new customer is, at best, only 20% whereas the success rate of selling to an existing customer, at worst, is 60%. And even if you think your services are generally one–off transactions (*they're not, by the way*), a happy customer who is willing to refer their friends, family, coworkers, and acquaintances to you can increase your profits by as much as 95%.

What's even more interesting is that these new, revolutionary marketing strategies like SEO and paid ads are reverting back to rewarding the original way people used to market a business—content. But it isn't just how much you're saying, it's what you're actually saying that matters. Stuffing a 30 blogs a week full of keywords and backlinks isn't effective anymore. Instead, it's quality information and a consistent message, which are the core components of what early marketers did to generate buzz, awareness, and referrals for their business.

Using internet tools to market your business isn't a complete reinvention of the wheel. It's an enhancement and an amplifier for the strategies that have been working for thousands of years. And now that you understand where we're coming from, you can better conceptualize our approach to content marketing and how it fits into your business's growth ecosystem.

Referrals and word of mouth marketing are still the best ways to bring in the best clients and customers. There's no need to abandon the strategies that have worked for thousands of years to grow your business. Instead, use the great technology you have at your disposal to make those strategies even more effective. This book aims to help you do that.

Chapter 2 ~ The Biggest Problem with Modern Marketing

For many years, traditional marketing theory has focused on the idea of a "marketing funnel." And for a long time, businesses and marketers thought this was the best (and perhaps only) way to successfully market a business. If you've ever launched a marketing campaign of your own or worked with a marketing company or consultant, then you're likely familiar with the concept of a marketing funnel. Although funnels can have different milestones, most funnels follow this general path:

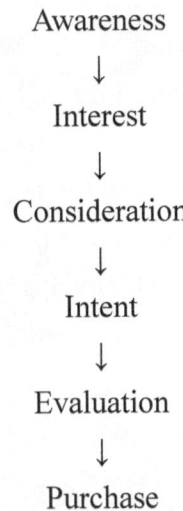

Awareness
↓
Interest
↓
Consideration
↓
Intent
↓
Evaluation
↓
Purchase

The leads you generate from a marketing campaign, whether that's from direct mail, cold calls, purchased email lists, paid ads, or something else, all usually start very cold at the top of the funnel in the "Awareness" stage. From there, whatever steps your marketing or sales team takes for the duration of the campaign (a series of email drips, phone calls, direct mail, etc.) should move that lead down the funnel, warming them up until they hopefully make a purchase by the end of the campaign.

But there's always been a gigantic flaw with marketing funnels and the campaigns that go with them—they end.

Most marketing companies don't see this—or if they do, they just don't care. That's because they're focused on the top of the funnel. Most marketing companies are just interested in helping you generate leads that *might* be qualified to work with your business. Once they've hit that metric, they're out! This might sound nice (they're doing their job, right?), but what it means is that the long-term success of your business doesn't matter to them.

But it matters to us, and that's honestly not a hollow, PR-appeasing statement we just flippantly make. We truly care how many clients the firms we work with bring in, AND we care how many they keep because it provides constant, unwavering validation that our strategy works. Looking at the marketing funnel, we knew there must be a better, more holistic marketing solution. So, we sat down and came up with a revolutionary strategy that helps law firms not only win clients, but also retain them, nurture them, and keep them engaged. We call it The Content Loop™.

What is The Content Loop™? The idea behind our proven process is pretty simple: The loop closes the end of the funnel so clients no longer "fall out" after you schedule them for the first time. Basically, we took the end of the funnel and stretched it around to connect back to the top. This loop is made possible by consistently putting out content, including blogs, videos, social media posts, e-newsletters, and website updates.

This flow of content creates ongoing touch points with your network—the leads, referrals, referral sources, clients, colleagues, strategic relationships, family, and friends—living inside the loop. When you keep up the flow, it keeps your brand top of mind and builds up your reputation over time so no lead, referral, or opportunity is missed. When we create our Content Loop™ for our clients we diversify the content and blast it out on all of the common channels so your marketing efforts reach everyone in your network: avid readers, video junkies, and social media surfers. Over time, you'll inevitably become a familiar, trusted brand.

When you build loops instead of funnels, it's impossible for your network to forget who you are and what you do. This method is proven to lower churn and strengthen relationships. And all of it is done with content. It's like the same word of mouth and branding that the ancient fish sauce company and winery took advantage of, but completely gacked out on steroids.

There's a Huge Opportunity for Even More Referrals!

We surveyed over 10,000 business owners and asked what percentage of their business comes from referrals. The results absolutely shocked us.

According to our results, only ⅓ of business owners get less than half of their business from referrals. Yikes.

Another somewhat shocking statistic was that 18% of respondents didn't actually know how much of their business came from referrals. We'll cover metrics later on in this book, but PLEASE PLEASE PLEASE start tracking your data if you're not already doing so. You'll have no idea about how to gauge the effectiveness of your marketing if you don't have any data to reference.

For now, though, let's stick with referrals. According to a study conducted by Texas Tech University, businesses are only getting about ⅓ of the referrals they should be. The study found that, on average, 83% of satisfied clients are willing to make referrals, but only 29% actually do it.

How would you like to double your business using only referrals? All you need to do is stay in touch.

If you consistently stay in touch with your current and past clients and remind them of what you do and how you can help, it makes a huge impact on your referrals. You need to consistently reach out to them and put your business's name and expertise front and center. This will increase your brand's awareness and keep it top of mind. That will inevitably increase your referrals without impacting the rest of your marketing budget.

Action Item: Calculate Your Referrals

Take a deep dive into your CRM and calculate how many of your clients have come from referrals over the last 12 months. (If you aren't even tracking that, it's time to build a system to do so!) Divide that number by the total number of clients you've worked with and see what percentage of your business comes from referrals. Unless 100% of your business comes from referral, you have room to make improvements.

Think of it this way: If you've just eaten at a restaurant and had an incredible meal, aren't you more likely to recommend that restaurant to a friend when they ask where they should go for dinner? Even driving by the restaurant and seeing the sign can have the same effect if you haven't eaten there in a while. The simple truth is, the more recently someone has used or interacted with a business, the more likely they are to recommend that business when the topic comes up in conversation.

The reality is that we're so bombarded with information on a daily basis that it's so easy to forget you, regardless of how great you think you are and well of a job you did.

Eat at this restaurant!

Watch that new show on Netflix!

Wear this!

Listen to this new song!

Watch this viral video!

Check what your relatives posted on Facebook!

Read this news story!

That's why keeping in touch (and doing it often) is so important towards driving those referrals. In the past, businesses relied on holiday and birthday cards to stay in touch with their clients and customers to satisfy their referral marketing, but in the hectic, fast–paced, digitally saturated world we live in today, that's not enough anymore.

Two Different Real Life Examples Highlighting the Power of Referrals

During one of our regular client check–ins, one of our clients told us a story that is every lawyer's worst nightmare. It all started when our client (we'll call him Justin) got a phone call.

"Hello!" said the person on the other end of the line. "I'm looking for a lawyer who can help me with a family law issue."

"Oh, I'm sorry!" Justin told the caller. "Family law isn't my specialty. But I know another lawyer who is excellent at it. Let me give you her name."

When Justin passed on the name of the other attorney, his caller gasped.

"Oh my gosh, I actually worked with her three months ago," they said. "I was very happy with her work and wanted to get in touch with her again, but I couldn't remember her name or figure out how to find her. So, I went online and found you instead!"

Justin's heart sank. He was thrilled that the caller had found him online and was inspired by the content we'd helped him create, but he also felt awful for his friend. This customer with a case worth thousands of dollars in repeat business and potential referrals had almost gotten away.

It's chilling to think you could be just like that family law attorney, losing clients without even knowing it despite being excellent at your job. If you're not getting 100% of the referrals you could be getting, then **you are just like that family law attorney**. The only question is exactly how much you've been losing.

And we're sure you're thinking, "How could that person so easily forget about an attorney who helped them through such a big legal issue in just three months? Wouldn't they have retained some sort of documentation, letterheads, or business cards?" If so, then you greatly underestimate how forgetful and disorganized the majority of people are.

And while we could turn this chapter into a philosophical debate over which issue should be fixed—your referral rate or society's attention span and organization—we'll end this story with this thought: The easiest thing to do in marketing (and in life) is to maintain an internal locus of control. What can you do to fix a problem or navigate a particular situation? Obviously, it's much easier for you to do everything you can to stay in touch with your audience than it is to teach everyone how to stay organized and remember something specific.

In our other example, one of our employees shared their referral experience with us during a company meeting. They told us they had gotten two speeding tickets within the last year. After each ticket, they opened their mailbox to find dozens of mailers from different local attorneys.

These attorneys were on the ball, and they were pursuing this lead hard. (If you're a personal injury or criminal defense attorney, you likely employ this same strategy.) Our team member estimated they received around 30 pieces of physical direct mail in total. But here's the kicker: *None of those attorneys got their business.*

Instead of picking a mailer out of the stack, our employee turned to their friends and family.

"Hey," they asked, "do you know any attorneys who do traffic tickets?"

The answer was "Yes!" In fact, they ended up using two separate referrals to handle their tickets because they were pulled over in two different cities (but let's try not to focus on that lead foot).

This story reinforces the idea that firms just don't spend enough time keeping in touch with their leads, clients, and referral partners and instead devote their energy and marketing dollars to bringing in new leads **despite it costing 5x more to acquire new business** than it does to stay in touch with your existing contacts.

The truth is that even today, the majority of people don't want to find their attorney (or accountant, or chiropractor, etc.) through a piece of mail or an online advertisement. They want a referral from someone they already know and trust. And you can only get those referrals by staying in touch—an opportunity many business owners miss out on. If you've ever let a lead walk out the door without following up or left a networking event with a business card you never added to your mailing list, then you're guilty of this neglect. And here's the thing—*even if a lead decides not to do business with you, it doesn't mean that they can still refer others to you.*

Now, we're not saying doing things like sending mailers, paying for SEO, or running online ads don't deserve to be part of your marketing strategy. They have their time and place. But they won't patch the biggest hole or create the same opportunities as simply nurturing your network, which includes your friends, family, colleagues, and connections (basically anyone you've spoken with or who follows you on social media) and, by extension, their friends, family, etc.

Now that we've made you feel awful about your marketing strategy, how exactly do you stay in touch with your contacts?

Chapter 3 ~ The Answer Is Content

You've probably heard the statement "Content Is King" before. But do you know why?

No matter where someone finds you—leads, referrals, people that are in your existing network, colleagues, people that find you online—they're going to engage with your content. It's the first interaction they have with your business. Because of this, the right content strategy makes all of your marketing work better.

If you have a good marketing strategy in place when someone provides you their contact information, they're going to hopefully get your email newsletter. Then they're going to be exposed to your blogs. Then they're going to check out your social media presence. See what's happening? Your content actually enhances and affects all of your marketing efforts whether they're online or offline, lead generation, or networking.

The right content strategy makes your marketing work and the right content strategy is going to position your firm as the expert, educate your audience, and help you stay top-of-mind. When those things happen, people think of you in their moment of need. You become the go-to expert, the leader, and the one that people want to work with.

That's why content is king. It makes all of your marketing work better because it affects every aspect of your marketing strategy, right down to people you meet while networking because those people are going to be exposed to your content and interact with it. From there, your content is going to keep you top of mind and is going to enhance your image and your reputation so that you become the expert that people want to work with.

What Kind of Content Should You Create?

There are two types of content that people want to read:

1. Content related to what you do and how you can help.
2. Content that helps them get to know you and your business on a personal level.

The first type is the most important. Sharing your knowledge in the form of tips, advice, and success stories is the best way to boost your reputation and position yourself as an expert. The more articles, videos, and podcasts you publish related to your business, the more knowledgeable and experienced you'll appear. People want to do business with experts!

The second type of content includes things like recommendations of other businesses you like, productivity or general life hacks you've discovered that work well for you, and social media posts with pictures of your family. Anything that will help readers get to know, like, and trust you falls into this category. We'd suggest centering 20% or less of your blogs, social media posts, and videos on personal topics. Keep at least 80% related to business.

We've also seen a third kind of content floating around out there, and it honestly makes us irrationally angry. You've probably seen it, too (or maybe you do this)—the emails or posts that have absolutely nothing to do with you or your business:

- Cookie recipes
- How to celebrate National Pokemon Day (or whatever offbeat holiday is coming up)

- Tips for Saving the Bees (or something equally as random even though your business and personal hobbies have nothing to do with those things)

The point is this—you are a lawyer, an accountant, a chiropractor, (insert profession here). You are NOT a source of news or human interest pieces. Let people visit Yahoo! or Buzzfeed for articles like that. If a topic isn't related to you or your business, skip it. Don't spend time on something that won't produce results!

How Much Content Is Too Much?

Every good business owner knows that content has value, whether it's in the form of social media posts, podcasts, blogs, emails, or videos. Consistent, relevant content is how you keep your brand and services top of mind and build up your expertise. But are you putting out enough content?

Probably not. In fact, however much content you're putting out could be increased exponentially.

How is that possible? Well, think about the environment we live in. Everywhere you go, no matter what you're doing, your smartphone connects you to a bottomless pool of information. In the past when you were sitting at the doctor's office waiting your turn, you were stuck with nothing to do but flip through the outdated *People* magazines on the waiting room coffee table. Now, you can pull out your phone and do just about anything.

You can scroll through social media, watch a video, listen to a podcast, or (and here's the kicker) look up a good lawyer, accountant, financial advisor, chiropractor, etc. Do you want to be educated? Do you want to be entertained? It's up to you.

Netflix, Disney Plus, and all of these other streaming services are viable because we're living in the golden age of content consumption! Our appetite for content is bottomless, and we plow through a mountain of it every day. That's why we're 100% sure your business isn't putting out enough social media posts, blogs, podcasts, and videos into the digital universe—it's pretty much impossible to put out too much content.

That being said, you can contribute to the growing culture. The more you feed into it, the more leads and referral sources you'll touch. When it comes to picking that first piece of content and multiplying it out across platforms and formats, remember the golden rule of content creation: **It doesn't have to be perfect. It just has to be good enough.**

Now, we're not saying you should put out volumes of bad content and spam everyone's timelines. That won't do anything but make you look bad. What we're saying is you shouldn't spend days or weeks agonizing over a particular post or article, trying to make it the best it can possibly be. Instead, churn out a post that's good enough and spend that extra time creating more posts or leveraging the one you just finished to reach more people.

Apart from perfectionism, another thing that slows down content creation is worrying about the ROI. In the world we live in right now, **ROI is not the end all, be all of content anymore**—we consume endlessly and erratically, and that makes it impossible to draw a straight line connecting the dots from the creation of content to the conversion of a lead. In our experience, a lot of the benefits of consistent, high-volume content are untraceable. For example, someone might read a post on your blog, then refer a friend to your firm without even telling that friend how they found you. That's a big point in favor of creating more content that won't show up in your ROI.

There is no such thing as too much content right now. There's no point where someone is going to look at how much you're putting out and say, "Stop! I can't take it!" But you can reach a point where you're making every smart move you can.

The best part is that you don't need to devote additional hours to putting out more content. Through simple repurposing and multiplication, you can take one piece of content and turn it into more than 50 different posts with just a little bit of work. See the steps below!

1. Record a 2–3 minute video explaining a concept or answering a common question you receive.

2. Upload that video to YouTube, Facebook, your personal LinkedIn profile, and your website.
*** 4 pieces of content created ***

3. Share the video on your company LinkedIn page, Google My Business, and Twitter.
*** 7 pieces of content created ***

4. Grab a 30–60 second clip from your video and share it to your Instagram and TikTok profiles.
*** 9 pieces of content created ***

5. Share the video again on your Facebook, Twitter, Google My Business, and both LinkedIn pages because

many people may not see it the first time because of all the other content they're consuming.
14 pieces of content created*

6. Rip the audio from your video and make it a podcast episode.

7. Post your podcast episode on your website, syndicate it to Apple Podcasts, Spotify, Pandora, iHeart, Amazon Podcasts, Google Podcasts, etc.
21 pieces of content created*

8. Grab a 30–60 second audio clip and share it on Facebook, Twitter, Google My Business, and both of your LinkedIn pages.
26 pieces of content created*

9. Get the audio transcribed, make some edits, and publish it as a blog post to your website.
27 pieces of content created*

10. Share the blog post on Facebook, Twitter, Google My Business, and both LinkedIn pages at least twice because many people may not see it the first time because of all the other content they're consuming.
37 pieces of content created*

11. Share that blog post on sites like Quora and Medium.
39 pieces of content created*

12. Take 2 or 3 key quotes from your blog and use a site like Canva to create graphics that you can post to Instagram, Facebook, Twitter, Google My Business, and both LinkedIn pages.
51 pieces of content created

13. Take your blog or your video (or both), and create an email newsletter to send to your contact list!
52 pieces of content created

If you're starting completely from scratch, there may be a little learning curve with some of the apps you need to use, but once you establish a system and develop a consistent rhythm, you and your team can create a well-oiled content machine with only a couple of hours of work. Think about all of the billable hours you can gain back by simply repurposing and multiplying a single piece of pillar content into dozens of usable pieces!

While the most aggressive branders and marketers would say to do this every day, we don't think you need to go that far. You can do this every week or have a themed content month where all of your content focuses on one topic.

How Will This Actually Help You?

At the very least, a solid content marketing foundation will make all of the other marketing you do work that much better. Remember those BASF commercials from the 1990s where their slogan at the end was always: "At BASF, we don't make a lot of the products you buy; we make a lot of the products you buy better"? That's what content marketing does for you at a *bare minimum.*

Here's a great example of this: A couple of years ago, one of our clients, a business attorney in Florida, sat next to a stranger on a plane. The two men got to talking about their work as you do when your legs are cramped and you're stuck breathing stale air. Eventually, they exchanged business cards and a handshake, then the plane landed and they went their separate ways. They never expected to speak again.

However, our client had hope! When he got back to his office, he added his travel companion's email address to his newsletter mailing list. Every month, our client's blogs and videos showed up in this guy's inbox. Months later, our client got a call out of the blue.

"I don't know if you remember me," said the voice on the other end. "But a year ago, we sat next to each other on a plane. I'm starting a business, and I need an attorney. I've been getting your newsletter, and I think you're the guy."

Best of all, there was no negotiating over the price of the service and no long sales consultation where our client had to sell anything. It was all ready to go. You don't get that with search engines.

That's how content can close a client. In our experience, attorneys and other business owners can market in a handful of ways: networking, email and print newsletters, pay per click, public speaking, ads on the radio, TV, social media…you get the picture. But if you were to map out all of the different types of marketing you do, then you'd realize that content is sitting at the center like a friendly spider in the middle of a big, sticky web. If you set up your marketing correctly, then no matter where someone enters your marketing system, they should eventually end up engaging with your content.

Let's go back to the airplane story. When our client handed over his business card, he was networking. **All of your marketing success starts with a networking strategy.** Without it, your marketing might as well be a tree in the forest that falls without anyone to hear it make a sound.

After networking, our client doubled down by sending his email newsletter to that lead. But it wasn't just the act of sending the email that made the difference, it was the content within that newsletter that convinced the entrepreneur he wanted to do business. The same is true in pay–per–click advertising. Once it drives a lead to your website, it's your blog entries, videos, and social media posts that reveal your expertise and seal the deal. If you have the right content strategy, then even a quick skim is enough to make the difference.

At least 75% of your future clients will interact with your content before they make an appointment, and the other 25% will still check it out before coming into the office. That inevitability is the #1 reason content can enhance your overall marketing. Content itself doesn't always create leads or potential new clients, but it's the ultimate enhancer of everything else you're doing.

There's another reason content is the most effective tool in your arsenal: It influences what people think about you and your firm. The more content you have and resources you provide, the more reputable and experienced you'll appear. Imagine you have a basic website with just your logo, bio, and a headshot, while your competitor down the street has all of the content bells and whistles: a blog, FAQ videos, a newsletter, a podcast, and more. Who looks like a more serious, reputable choice?

The truth is that content builds and reinforces your reputation and expertise. But what matters most is that it's the spider in the center of the web: If your content is targeted and robust, then it will improve all of your other marketing efforts because they're all connected. Content doesn't live in a vacuum and neither does your other marketing!

The improvement your content creates may not translate directly to more clients. Instead, it might mean more consultations, that your clients are more confident in you, or that the leads you close are worth twice as much. Whatever the specific outcome, though, it's sure to be positive.

Remember, marketing can only bring prospective clients to your door. It's still your responsibility to close the deal.

Content Creates More Referrals

Referrals are the bread and butter of almost every small business from legal to financial to home services and more. We're sure you get a bunch of them, but you're probably missing out on more than you realize. Remember that Texas Tech survey we mentioned earlier in this book? **You can literally double the number of referrals you're receiving right now and still have room to get more.** How much would doubling your referrals help your business right now?

A great content strategy can help you solve that problem! By putting out the right content and leveraging it correctly, We've seen law firms, accountants, architectural firms, real estate agents, and more increase and even double their referrals.

Unfortunately, one of the biggest reasons business owners miss out on referrals is that they aren't consistently staying in touch with their past clients and referral partners. (Have we beaten this dead horse enough yet?) Your method of reaching out doesn't even need to be print or digital mail. Social media, for example, was designed specifically for this purpose! Sure, you can use it to reach out to new people, but first and foremost, you should use it to keep in touch with your existing network. Every piece of content you share via social media, email, or print is a touchpoint that reminds your audience of who you are and what you do, making them more likely to think of you when it's referral time.

But to really maximize your referrals, you need to focus not only on who your content is for, but what it's saying about you. The content you put out should be focused specifically on the type of work you do and aim to answer common questions your clients have. In this case, being entertaining isn't nearly as important as being informative.

Don't focus your content and messaging on your past performance; instead, let client testimonials do that for you. Instead, focus on providing commentary, insights, and practical guidance in a variety of ways in your industry. **Show how you can help the next person, not how you performed with the last one.**

If your content is relevant to your services, even a quick title scan should remind readers of what to refer you for. Your old clients are a lot more likely to remember that you do estate planning if they see an email about it in their inbox, and that will make it easier for the lightbulb to go off in their head when a family member, friend, or colleague needs help with it. On top of reminding readers what you do so that they know who to point your way, educational content positions you as the expert in your field. If you're sharing knowledge, people will perceive you as knowledgeable, and every social media post, website blog, and email newsletter will remind them of it.

Chapter 4 ~ Identifying Your Perfect Client

Your marketing playbook is absolutely worthless if you have no real idea as to who you're actually marketing to. What's even worse is if someone asks who your target market is and you answer "everyone." Meredith Hill said it best when she said "When you speak to everyone, you speak to no one."

Are you familiar with the concept of "door law"? If you're a lawyer, you might be. It's the oldest trap in the lawyer book and a myth that's run many freshly minted attorneys into the ground before they even got started. Practicing "door law" means leaving your door open to any client who wants to walk through it.

And it's not just for lawyers. You can be a door accountant, a door financial advisor, etc. Instead of specializing, these business owners take every call, attempting to be everything to everyone in a desperate bid for steady cash flow.

Despite it being an awful approach to business, it's a strategy many business owners have used at some point in their careers in order to get by. We completely understand why people choose this approach. If you're a solo operation, the simple truth is that you need money, and someone has probably told you that opening your door to everyone is the key to earning it, especially in the first years of your business. To be completely honest with you, we used to do that in the early days of Spotlight Branding. We offered practically every marketing service under the sun as a way to get started before we realized something very important.

We thought (as do countless other small businesses) that the best way to maximize profits is to cast the net of potential clients as wide as possible. We worked with car dealers, lenders, a radio show, non–

profits, and even an international appliance company. After a few years of trying to be everything to everyone, we realized that we should have been doing the opposite: **The best way to maximize your profitability is to choose a niche.**

Discarding a majority of your overall industry or geographic audience might seem counterintuitive, but in our years of working with lawyers, we've seen proof that it's the most effective strategy for growth. When you niche down, these five things will happen to boost your revenue:

1. Your credibility will go up

People want to work with specialists, and if you specialize, your experience will heighten your reputation and credibility in your field. Think of it this way: Who would you rather have fix your roof? A dedicated roof repairman who spends 40 hours a week with shingles or an all-around handyman who would be just as happy unclogging your sink? Odds are you'd choose the roof repairman because you'd trust them to do the job right.

2. You'll have a basis to raise your rates

This goes hand in hand with the previous point. If you're a specialist, you'll command higher rates because you'll be seen as more experienced, unique, and trustworthy. Rather than the previous analogy of the roof repair, ask yourself this: "If I needed brain surgery, how much more money would I pay to have a brain surgeon do it instead of a general practitioner?" Cost probably wouldn't matter much, right?

3. You'll have less competition

If you try to include every product or practice area into your business, you'll be competing with every other generalist and specialist in your city doing the same thing. However, if you niche down, you'll cut that competition down by a lot. Depending on where you're located and how wisely you choose your specialty, you could even eliminate competition altogether by becoming the only specialist in your field.

4. Your marketing will get easier

When you serve everyone, "everyone" becomes your target demographic. This makes advertising difficult because you can't tailor your messaging to the needs, fears, and desires of a particular group or use the resources provided by other specialists to find them because you risk alienating the rest of your audience. But when you choose a niche, your marketing becomes much more efficient. You'll know exactly who to target and you won't waste money catering to people who aren't interested in your services.

5. You'll earn more referrals

Yeah, we're still talking about referrals! If you met someone who loved cooking and talked your ear off about it, odds are you'd be more likely to think of them when the word "cooking" came up in conversation than you'd be to think about someone who only mentioned the hobby in passing. The same thing works for your business. Specialists are more memorable and more likely to pop into the minds of their past clients when their niche comes up. Because of that, if you specialize in a focused area, odds are your referrals will increase because you become known as THE guy or gal who handles a specific issue, fixes a specific problem, or provides a specific solution.

In order to truly leave behind the work you hate doing and start hooking your dream clients, the first thing you need to do is niche down. Maybe your niche is in the area of law/finance/etc. you enjoy most. Maybe it's something you're fantastic at. Or maybe it's what's most profitable for you. The definition is up to you—what's important is that you narrow it down.

Action Item: Discover Your Niche

Becoming the expert means niching down and focusing on one or two things you're exceptionally good at. Additionally, niching down makes it easier for people to know what kind of business to refer to you. Think about your answers to the questions below. If you start to see a pattern emerge, it may be time to niche down and really focus on that particular area of your business.

1. What do I actually enjoy doing?
2. What do I do exceptionally well?
3. What do I receive the most praise for?
4. Why do potential clients/customers come to my business?
5. How much of my marketing is focused on what I actually enjoy doing?

Hopefully we've convinced you that you no longer have to take every single client that walks through your door. On the surface, it may seem like an easy way to keep a steady stream of business, but it makes marketing your business so much harder because you have to satisfy all of the different areas of work you do, on top of staying competitive with all of the other businesses who do the same work or provide the same service.

Once you've found your niche, it's time to identify your ideal client. Perhaps you don't want to work with every single person who, for example, needs to build a retirement account. Maybe you want someone with a certain income, education, or lifestyle (more on that in a bit).

When you have your ideal client figured out, you can begin to focus your marketing messages and content around that profile. There are a lot of different ways to do this from an advertising and lead–generation standpoint, but your best tool for attracting the clients you want is by concentrating the content you create. All of the content marketing you do, whether it's via your blog, videos, podcast, or social media, should be created with your ideal client in mind.

To do that, ask yourself: "What circumstances are they in? What are their questions and concerns? What keeps them up at night?"

Then, answer those questions with content. The more attention you pay to a particular type of client in your marketing, the more you're going to attract it. It's not rocket science, but you wouldn't believe how many business owners leave this strategy on the table!

Here's an example of how all of this comes together: Dave is an estate planning attorney who, until now, has taken every client who walks through his door looking for an estate plan. However, he'd really like to specialize in high net worth estate planning. To get there, he starts focusing on wealthier individuals in his content.

He immediately stops putting out blogs about affordable estate planning options for low–income households. Instead, he talks about how an estate plan can help someone pass on their wealth or how to include provisions for assets like passive income properties. By discussing these things, it looks like Dave specializes in those specific needs, which is the first step towards making specialization a reality.

Once you appear to be the expert, you'll draw in clients looking to work with the best. But as easy as that sounds, there's a little more to it. We're not actually living in *Field of Dreams*. It's not always true that "if you build it, they will come."

You still need to pursue other marketing avenues to leave those undesirable clients behind for good like networking with referral sources and finding new ways to reach your audience. These extra strategies are the middle of the equation, but content is both the beginning and the end. It's how you reach people and it's where new leads always end up landing.

The key takeaway here though is that **you don't have to settle.** The idea that there won't be enough business for you if you specialize is a total myth. If you still need proof, consider this: One of our clients works only tractor trailer accident cases and their business is booming. Another left behind family law because it made them miserable. Since their content was focused on the type of work they enjoyed doing the most, their business didn't suffer at all. Even if you're currently in a position where you're taking every customer/client/patient that comes through your door, you can still make this pivot yourself and keep moving forward.

In review, when it comes to getting the most out of your content playbook, make sure you're doing the following: First, pinpoint your ideal client, and don't miss the details. A lot of business owners miss the bullseye when it comes to identifying their target market, and the first problem is that they don't sit down and put thought into exactly who they're looking for. Obviously, your generic audience is "people who need your services," but you can go deeper than that.

If you're an accountant, for example, consider which specific group needs your help. Are they business owners? People with families? Why not take it a step further and say middle-income or wealthy families? Then, think about the gender, age, and even hobbies of those people. Don't try to be everything to everyone. Instead, ask yourself, "Who are my services/products the ideal solution for?" and zero in on those groups.

Second, ask yourself, "Who has gathered these people together already?" This step is critical and will save you a massive amount of time. Once you've identified your target market, the next big question is how you'll reach them.

How will you drive these perfect clients to your website? How will you get them to dial your phone number or even realize that you exist? Well, it's actually easier than you think. Other business owners have already done the legwork for you, all you need to do is profit from it.

Here's what we mean. Say you're a family law attorney. Your target demographic probably includes families and couples who are either already getting divorced or might be interested in splitting. So ask yourself, "Who has gathered those people already?" Marriage counselors have, CPAs have, and maybe even local women's shelters! If you can connect with those groups, they can become your referral partners.

You can also target clients based on their hobbies and interests, which include both virtual meeting places and in-person locations. An accountant catering to small business owners, for example, might look for clients at the Chamber of Commerce, in the subscriber listings of *Entrepreneur* magazine, or on a local Facebook group for business owners.

Lastly, share a message that resonates. To bring these clients into your office, you need to share a specific, targeted message that resonates with them on a logical and emotional level. (For more information on how to do that, check out *Building a StoryBrand* by Donald Miller.) This is where knowing your demographic to a T comes in handy. Once you know who needs your services/products and why, you can cater your services to their needs and even send it out into the spaces—including the websites, podcasts, and print publications—they frequent.

Now that you have the understanding you need for your content marketing playbook, it's time to (finally) dive in. The next few chapters will cover the various elements of your playbook so that everything we've discussed so far (content multiplication, The Content Loop™, and more) will create a complete marketing picture for you and your business.

Action Item: Identify Your Perfect Client

Use these key identifiers below to figure out the exact kind of person you want to work with. In other words, if your perfect client walked through your door right now, what characteristics/traits would they possess?

Age:	Gender:	Ethnicity:
Income:	Occupation:	Education:
Marital Status:	Family Size:	Location:
Religion:	Media Consumption	Places They Visit:
Hobbies:	Goals/Challenges:	Other:

NOTE: For B2B businesses, think about additional identifiers like your clientele's industry, years in operation, revenue, expected growth, profit, and number of employees.

Chapter 5 ~ Your Website: Your Business's First Impression

Twenty years ago, business owners invested the bulk of their time and attention into how their office/storefront looked. After all, that first step into a business space was usually the first interaction a person would have with that business. Not anymore.

Regardless of how someone hears about your business, they will search for you online. There are several studies out there you can reference, but the general consensus is that 70–80% of people look at a company's website before making a purchase decision. That means your website needs to make a spectacular first impression if you want to even have a chance of winning someone's business.

But before we get into how to do that, we want to make something crystal clear: **Just because people are searching for your business online doesn't mean you have to invest in SEO.** When people hear about your business, they're going to search specifically for your name or your firm's name. They aren't going to be doing generic searches like "family lawyer near me" or "CPA in Boston."

Those people may still go to Google and search for "Smith Law Firm," but at that point, SEO doesn't matter. When you're searching for something that specific, Google is smart enough to find the exact business you're looking for (assuming there aren't thousands of "Smith Law Firms" in your city, and chances are there aren't).

Despite still being easily findable and indexed in search engines, however, this is a huge mistake many business owners make. Their websites are built for search bots rather than the human beings that are going to hire them.

Think about this: Would you make an emotional love confession to your toothbrush? Would you tell your favorite joke to a glass of water? If you answered "no" twice, take a minute to think about why those answers were so easy, and yet so many business owners (and maybe even you) don't bat an eye about marketing to search engine bots.

We'll have a chapter devoted to SEO later on, but for now we'll leave it at this: The SEO landscape is so competitive that you can gamble away thousands of dollars and hours without any return (and as a small business, you already have a limited amount of money to gamble away). But when you focus on people, you're guaranteed to accomplish your goal of staying in touch and keeping your business top of mind.

So how do you cater your website to humans? Surely you know what we're going to say, right? You use content!

By using content, you can put yourself in your clients' shoes, answer their questions, and tell them what they want to hear. You can make your business relatable and build your credibility. This is what makes content such a valuable marketing tool. But when you shift your focus away from helpful, meaningful information in favor of stuffing pages full of keywords, you lose that advantage.

Ultimately, your toothbrush, a glass of water, and search engines have one key thing in common: None of them are your target audience. They aren't the ones who will ultimately decide to accept your love, laugh at your joke, or do business with you. So instead of wasting your money and time targeting robots, speak to the people you really care about: your clients, leads, and referral partners.

So what does that look like and how does your website make a difference?

For starters, many business owners in white collar industries deal with a lack of trust. Whether people think you're an ambulance chasing lawyer or a greedy financial advisor who takes more money in fees than what the client gets in return on their investments (or something else), trust is a huge factor, especially among Millennials and younger generations. The best and easiest way to eliminate those stigmas is to offer free information on your website.

But before we get into what that includes, we want to tell you that your website absolutely should be more than just a couple of pages with your contact info, the services you provide, and simply saying "we can help." You need to highlight your expertise, address your visitors' concerns, and make an emotional connection with them through the imagery and content that exists on your website.

With that in mind, here are four things that are an absolute must-have on your website:

1. A regularly updated blog

Having a regularly maintained blog with evergreen topics that cover your areas of expertise is a great way to provide information on your website. You don't have to recreate chapters from your college textbooks, but you can provide basic, surface–level overviews of a given issue and show that you're the expert they can trust.

2. A robust video library

For people who prefer watching videos to reading text, a video library is another great way to provide free information. Even more, video has a couple of psychological benefits that blogs can't provide:

> A. First, videos break down any sort of barrier that exists between you and the client where they lose any intimidation they felt by you. They can now feel more

comfortable around you knowing they can put a face and a sound to your name.

B. Second, videos mentally prepare viewers for when they take the next step and come into your office for the consultation. Even if it's just slightly, that extra preparation will make your job easier.

3. A newsletter signup

Whether you have an email or print newsletter campaign, make sure there's a way people can opt into it on your website. Then, if you're doing your marketing right, they'll receive your latest blog or video (or both!) in your next newsletter without them ever having to regularly check your website.

4. A complimentary download

This is a great way to capture leads on your website. Having a free download, such as a white paper or ebook, is arguably the biggest credibility booster you can have on your website. And here's the thing: You don't need to actually write a full-length book or legal brief. You can take one of your most evergreen blogs, expand it a little bit, and turn it into a free download. Anything more than 1,500 words becomes laborious for the reader. (You can also provide a checklist or a worksheet that leads can interact with and fill out if it's appropriate for your particular niche.)

If your website lacks one or all of these free resources, you risk having a website that isn't living up to its fullest potential. But maybe you have all of these things. If so, great! Here are some additional items you can add to your website to make it even better.

1. Chat functionality

Those chat boxes you see in the corner of many websites have been shown to increase conversion by upwards of 33%. Whether you use an app that allows you or someone in your office to speak to visitors directly, you outsource it, or you have an AI bot with predetermined codes, these have been proven to improve your website's conversion rate. You can even incorporate text messaging (which people are becoming more and more comfortable with to communicate with businesses) into these plugins to provide a more direct interaction.

2. Retargeting pixel

If you're running pay–per–click (PPC) ads or just want to target people who have visited your website with specific social media posts, you can add a pixel code to your website that will then generate an audience that will see your content. Unless you're a marketing aficionado, this one is best left to a marketing expert, as there are several steps in this process both on the backend of your website and on the platforms where you're creating the custom/targeted audiences. Regardless, it could be a great way to continue getting in front of people who have visited your website.

3. Online scheduling

Want to make it easier for people to book consultations with you? Skip the contact forms and having your receptionist reach out to schedule a consultation. Instead, integrate your calendar with an app like Calendly, You Can Book Me, or others and streamline your booking process!

4. Mobile optimization

It's absolutely shocking how many small business websites don't work well on mobile devices even though that's where the bulk of web traffic comes from these days. If your website is more than five years old, there's a good chance that it doesn't load properly on phones or tablets. If someone is searching for an attorney/accountant/etc. and finds a clunky, broken website on their phone, they're likely not going to hire you.

Your website can be a great marketing tool on its own, but adding these extra bells and whistles can really put it to work for you and make things easier.

But here's the key: Your website is NOT a thing you set and forget. It needs to be consistently audited and updated. The restaurant industry is notorious for failing to do this.

Think about the last time you went online to order takeout food or just look at the menu. How was the experience? Did you put your order in without a hitch, or were you frustrated by the restaurant's outdated website, malfunctioning plugins, and counterintuitive ordering process? How many times have you tried to get basic information from a restaurant's website that was so frustrating that you said "Screw it!" and ordered something else through DoorDash instead?

Unfortunately, this problem isn't exclusive to restaurants. If you haven't updated your firm's website in a few years, YOU could be the one making people want to handle their legal issues, their taxes, their investments, etc. on their own by going to one of the many DIY sites that exist today. To win over clients and keep up your firm's image and reputation, you need to refresh your website regularly. Here are three big reasons to stay on top of those updates:

For starters, digital trends change. The looks considered eye-catching, popular, and modern online change just as often as what's "in" on the runway. What impressed visitors years ago might look awful today and vice versa. In 2021, asymmetrical website layouts are in style—who the heck would have predicted that in 2016? Updating your website regularly shows that you're keeping up with the times, and that's a reflection of your firm's credibility and attention to detail.

Additionally, the functionality of your website can fall apart. Think of your website like a car. As soon as you drive a new vehicle off the lot, its value goes down, and it keeps depreciating over time. After 10 years, your turn signals are sticky, your glove compartment won't close, and you have stubborn stains on your leather seats. The same thing will happen with your website, but much faster. A decade in car time is like two years online.

Websites have dozens of moving pieces and parts, and many of those plugins and integrations aren't native to the website itself. They get separate updates, and over time, they become incompatible or stop working entirely. Without regular full-site refreshes, entire sections of your website can become defunct. But when you update your website regularly, you can fix those issues and add cutting-edge features.

Lastly, outdated websites can misrepresent your business. Think about what your business looked like at the time your website was created. How many people were on your team? What did your branding and logo look like?

Odds are if your website is more than two years old, some or all of those things have changed. The COVID-19 pandemic forced thousands of business owners to pivot and update their messaging. If you haven't made those changes on your website, you're misrepresenting your brand and missing out on clients who could be ideal fits for you.

Your website needs to reflect the current you, not the old you. A refresh can make that happen and bring in an influx of consultations.

Tips for Working with a Web Designer

Unless you have professional experience designing a website (and we mean more than just spending a couple of hours on WordPress or Wix), then you should put your website in the hands of someone who does this sort of thing for a living. Before you make your final selection, make sure you ask a potential designer these five questions first.

1. Do I get to keep my website?

Many marketing companies actually don't let you keep your website when you decide to terminate your relationship with them. Other companies who build websites on their own proprietary platform may hand over the keys when you leave, but your website will likely break or begin to perform differently when you move it to a new host like GoDaddy or BlueHost. Make sure you understand what happens if you decide to end your relationship with your vendor.

2. Do I pay extra for needing changes to my website?

Watch out for this one! Many companies charge an hourly rate to make website changes. For example, one of our clients had her website with a different company. She requested a new page to be added, and they quoted her for four hours of work, which would have cost her over $200! (We went in and made the change for her in 15 minutes for free.) The moral of the story is to make sure what (if any) ongoing maintenance is included.

3. How long will it take to build my website?

Be wary of web design companies who promise to build your website in a week, a few days, or even 24 hours. These websites will either be super basic, something you could have done yourself for free, or a standard template website that could look exactly like any number of websites (including your competitor's) out there. Remember—the best websites take time to create because they're custom designed and programmed. If they're also writing the content for you (which we'll discuss next), that's also some added time to the project.

4. Do you create my website copy, or do I have to provide it?

If you're one of the few business owners that won't obsess over your writing and try your hardest to make it absolutely perfect, it's best to let your web design company write the content for you. However, make sure you understand their strategy. Are they going to be writing for the humans who visit your website, or will they be catering to search bots by forcing several keywords into your copy and disrupting the flow?

You also need to know whether or not the content being provided will be unique to your business. Syndicated content doesn't accomplish much and, depending on your business's goals, could do more harm than good. Shockingly enough, we've seen websites that were built by the same designer that contain the exact same web copy. Make sure your designer is going to create content that is unique to you and your business alone.

5. Do you provide hosting and security?

Make sure you understand your responsibilities here. Many companies just design a website and then rely on you to figure out where to put it, like GoDaddy, HostGator, etc. Alternatively, look for a company that provides the hosting and security for you, and see whether or not your website is fully covered in the event of a breach or a hack. Even the most secure websites in the world can fall victim to breakdowns, server downtime, or hackers, but very few hosting providers will help you undo any damage and get your website back to normal—at least not without charging a hefty fee.

6. How much experience do you have working with my specific industry?

Are you going to be working with a local designer with a portfolio that covers everything from restaurants to general contractors to lawyers? If so, that may mean that they don't specialize in your industry and may not be fully aware of how it works. Look for a designer that has experience working with other businesses in your specific industry. After all, a website for a white–collar professional will look very different from a website geared towards the restaurant industry.

7. Do you work well with other vendors?

While working with a one–stop shop for all of your marketing needs is certainly convenient, you'll see better results by having experts in various concentrations of marketing work together on your strategy. Unfortunately, some website designers don't play well with others and make it difficult (or downright impossible) for other vendors (or even your own staff) to make changes or implement improvements to your website. Make sure you set clear expectations if you'll have multiple vendors working with you and that everyone shares resources and makes each others' jobs easy.

Action Item: The Website Audit

Go to your website right now and answer these following questions:

1. Do I have a blog and has it been consistently updated?
2. Do I have videos where I answer my audience's common questions?
3. Do I have a free download?
4. Do I have a newsletter signup?
5. Is it clear what I even do?
6. Is it easy and obvious how to get in touch with me?
7. Are the images serving a purpose or are they just placeholders?
8. How does my website look when I try to access it on my smartphone?
9. In what year did this version of my website go live?
10. Do I have all of the back end and hosting login credentials I need in case of an emergency?

If you answered "no" to any of question 1–6, you should get to work. If the last four questions yielded disheartening answers, it's time to get your website redesigned.

Chapter 6 ~ Blogging: Your Pillar Content Starting Point

Now that you understand what makes a great website, let's dive into the specific content–related elements of your playbook. If you aren't comfortable in front of a camera or the thought of becoming an amateur audio engineer for your podcast seems too daunting right now (though we'll discuss these next!), you need to at least have a blog on your website. Blogging is the classic digital content medium and one that still provides a ton of benefits for your firm.

Many business owners (especially lawyers) make the mistake of having their blog be a news hub where they either brag about things they've done or provide a small (generally irrelevant) update to something specific to their industry. If that's you, **you're wasting your time**. Sure, there is value in letting people know you've done something good or that laws have changed, but your blog isn't the place for that.

The other problem is that writing blog posts can be daunting, and many business owners (especially lawyers, accountants, and financial pros) often end up poring over their articles in hopes of making it perfect. Before they know it, they've spent four hours on something that realistically only should have taken a quarter of that time. That's part of the reason so many business owners hire third–party vendors like us to write blogs for them.

That said, we're ready to let you in on a little secret: Writing blog posts really isn't that difficult. Seriously! All of the problems around blogging come from a stubbornness to make it perfect by diving deep into the weeds and covering the most minute details of whatever concept you're writing about. It doesn't have to be that way.

The Spotlight Branding Blogging Formula

Blogging is one of Spotlight Branding's oldest services, and having blogged for businesses for more than 10 years, we've perfected the process. Now, we're giving it to you!

1. Choose a topic

Admittedly, this is the hardest part, and we'll spend the most time on this point because of that. If you're struggling to figure out what to write about, the simplest thing to do is to think about the questions your clients ask you on a regular basis or the challenges they face. From there, list out the answers/solutions.

But with so much knowledge rattling around in your head, it can be tough to know what would appeal to the average reader. So whether you have a list of hundreds of topics you're trying to cull or you still aren't sure where to start, try one of these two methods.

First, you can reverse engineer a common scenario. Think of a situation that your average client might find themselves in. If you deal with taxes, your topic could revolve around your audience receiving a letter from the IRS.

When that letter comes in, what's the first question your audience is likely to have? Maybe it's, "Is this letter really from the IRS?" Write that question down and BAM!, you have a blog topic: "3 Ways to Tell If Your IRS Letter Is Legitimate."

And yes, we realize this topic seems incredibly oversimplified, but remember—your audience doesn't have near as much detailed and specific knowledge as you do. Assume they don't know anything (because chances are, they actually don't). Cover the most elementary topics first before you start getting into the weeds.

This strategy works in practically every industry from legal to accounting to home repair. Simply imagine yourself in your clients' shoes and answer their burning questions. This will reassure your readers you're the right person to clear up their confusion and allay their fears.

The other method of topic creation is using the multiplier effect. Once you have a single question or scenario in mind, you can easily spin it into more! Take the previous example of the IRS letter—obviously your audience won't only be asking themselves if their letter is legitimate.

Once they open the letter, they might have other questions like, "What type of IRS letter is this? What other kinds of letters does the IRS send? Why does the IRS use this particular language? What does this term mean?" Any of those queries could become a relevant blog post. Don't worry about your topics overlapping, either—repetition just reinforces your expertise.

While answering questions like that might seem basic, that's what people care about most. They want to know that you've mastered your field and can help people in common situations like the one they're in. Even more—especially when it comes to blogging—your audience doesn't want (and doesn't have the attention span) to take a deep dive of every single topic. Keep these things surface level.

Pretend someone walked up to you on the street and asked a question. What would your 60-second answer be? That's the approach you take to your blog posts (and your videos). If you really want to scratch that deep dive itch and really show off, use a different medium like podcasting.

Once you have your topic, the rest is actually pretty easy!

2. Create a short outline

To map out your blog post, choose 2–4 main points you'd like to make about the topic you picked and write them down. If you're unsure, imagine you're having a conversation with someone (not in your industry) about the topic at hand. What are the most important things you'd want them to know?

3. Flesh out your outline point by point

To create the body of your article, simply turn each of your main points into a paragraph. As you do this, remember that you're not writing for an industry textbook! Aim for generic, practical advice and basic tips. That way you'll avoid confusing your readers and keep your content evergreen. After all, if a minute detail in the law or procedure changes, you don't want to hunt down all of your old blog posts and make revisions, that's why surface level advice gets the job done!

4. Add an introduction and conclusion

That's right, this is just like what you learned in school. In your introduction, make sure you include something interesting or important to hook the reader, and don't forget to plug your contact information in the conclusion.

5. Title it!

In today's world, there's a lot of pressure to come up with creative, witty titles. But in our experience, the best titles are straightforward and to the point. You want a reader to glance at your title and know immediately both what the article is about and what you do. If you can add a little sparkle, too, even better.

Notice how our formula didn't include a point to edit, edit, and edit some more? While you want to skim through your article to make sure you didn't make any spelling or grammatical mistakes, you don't need to pore over it multiple times with a fine-toothed comb to cover every little detail. Remember, just because you want to look like an expert doesn't mean your content needs to be expert level by **your** standards. The average Joe's opinion of expert content isn't the same as yours or an industry peer's. Your goal also should not be to impress your industry peers because they are not your target audience.

Think about it like this: If Joe is in the market for an estate planning lawyer, for example, he won't be interested in reading about the intricacies of Spousal Lifetime Access Trusts. A hyper-specific article full of legalese will be a turnoff. Instead, he'd rather read a simple blog like, "3 Quick Tips for Creating a Will: Millionaire's Edition."

Keeping your content simple will make it more effective and save you time and effort. Here are a few final things to keep in mind when you sit down to write:

- Leave out the industry jargon. It might make you look smart, but your target audience won't get it. (You don't need to impress your industry peers.)
- Include practical advice. This will make your content worth reading.
- Make it scannable. Most people won't read an article all the way through, so include elements like bullets and subheadings for maximum impact.

Action Item: Create 10 Blog Topics

Use the prompts below to frame your next blog. If you'd like some additional help with your specific industry, we have included some sample topics from a few industries below this table to help you out!

An Introduction to…	X Myths About…
The Do's and Don'ts of…	X Questions to Ask…
How to…	X Reasons…
Step–by–Step Guide to…	Checklist
A Brief Overview of…	Q&A Style

Chiropractic:
- Benefits
- Nutrition
- Posture
- Stretching
- Subluxations

Construction/Engineering:
- Bids
- Contracts
- Disputes
- Retainage
- Scope of work issues

CPAs / Accountants:
- Budgeting tips
- Deductions vs. credits
- IRS audits
- Offer–in–Compromise
- Offshore accounts

Financial Professionals:
- Cryptocurrency
- Investing tips
- Retirement accounts
- Retirement saving
- Stocks/Bonds/ETFs

Home Services:
- Easy repairs
- Improvement tips
- Landscaping tips
- Mistakes to avoid
- Winterizing

Legal – Criminal Law:
- Arrest process
- Explanation of various charges
- Plea types
- Rights when pulled over
- Trial process

Legal – Immigration Law:
- All of the various visas
- Deportation
- Green Cards
- ICE
- Naturalization

Real Estate:
- Closing process/costs
- Disclosures
- Maximizing property value
- Short sales
- Title search

Legal – Estate Planning:
- All of the various trusts
- Estate taxes
- Powers of Attorney
- Probate
- Wills

Legal – Family Law:
- Child custody
- Child support
- Divorce
- Financial preparation
- Talking to your kids

Chapter 7 ~ Video: The Most Versatile Pillar Content

We've already discussed video in terms of content multiplication and getting the most out of it, so this chapter will be devoted to making those videos look great. Videos are an ideal way to reach current and potential clients. According to WordStream, people spend about ⅓ of their time online watching videos, and Forbes reports that over half a billion people watch videos on Facebook alone every single day.

Arguably the biggest hesitation we hear from clients is that they don't like how they look on camera. And that's understandable, since many of us are self-conscious about our appearance or the way our voice sounds. However, if your videos are part of your marketing, you're showing off exactly what people will see and hear when they meet you in person. Think of it as a consultation before the actual consultation.

Video can be a powerful marketing tool that not only allows you to show off your knowledge and expertise, but breaks down any preconceived notions that people may have about meeting you. However, if you're still on the fence, here are a two quick tips to get started.

1. Be yourself

It can be tempting to fall into a character based on your industry. Perhaps you think sounding firm and aggressive will make viewers believe "you mean business." Maybe you want to take a more compassionate, heartfelt tone.

If that isn't how you speak to prospective clients during a consultation, you don't need to do it in your videos. You don't need to put on a show or pretend to be something you're not. Simply speak with the same cadence you would as if that viewer were standing face to face with you at that moment.

In fact, the more natural you sound, the more of an expert you appear to be because you aren't forcing things or searching for the right words. You already know what you're talking about so you don't have to project a false air of sincerity. People can sniff out an acting job quickly, so your natural cadence (no matter how awkward you think you sound) makes your videos genuine and an excellent display of your expertise.

Perhaps most importantly, viewers aren't looking to be entertained by your videos; they're looking for answers. The more comfortable you are in your own skin, the more people will be drawn to you and believe what you have to say.

2. Give an authentic experience

Think about how the videos will look. If at all possible, shoot them somewhere in your office. If your office is too cluttered (or, alternatively, practically empty), a well-decorated and furnished lobby or conference room will work too.

Think about the lighting as well. Find a place with softer lights instead of the standard office fluorescent bulbs (more on this in a bit). A videographer may be able to bring studio lights, but keeping things as similar as they would when someone comes to see you in person is ideal.

Finally, think about your outfit. If you don't typically wear a suit at the office, don't wear one during your video shoot. It's all about giving the viewer the same experience and feeling of being in your office.

So what makes for a great video? In our experience, FAQ videos are the most effective type of video marketing you can create because it focuses on building relationships by allowing you to answer the questions your clients and leads are already asking. And sure, you can have one of those fancy, high-production, theatrical brand videos on your website, but FAQ videos really allow you to show off your expertise in a way those brand videos can't. So, how can you make FAQ videos for your business and cash in on that client-converting power?

Well, you have two options. First, you could outsource the process by hiring a professional film crew to set up the lighting, shoot the footage, and edit it for you. We do this all the time for our clients, but it's absolutely NOT necessary for success. The second option is to do it yourself, and we're going to show you how.

1. Gather your equipment

While moviemakers and vloggers have advanced equipment to make them look and sound great, you can make a good looking video without blowing your budget. In this instance when we say "equipment," we really just mean your smartphone. Each new smartphone that hits the market gets closer and closer to replicating the same audio and visual quality of a DSLR camera. We also live in a culture where selfie videos with imperfect sound quality are ubiquitous, and you'll even get points for being more real and approachable in your videos. That said, if you want to go above and beyond, then you can easily buy a smartphone tripod and clip-on microphone.

Next comes your lighting. Shine a lamp toward the wall facing you to softly illuminate your face and turn on a light behind you to create depth. Good sound quality can be just as simple to achieve. Rather than rely on your computer or laptop's microphone system, plug in your AirPods or headphones. These items often have built-in microphones that better capture your voice due to their proximity to your face.

2. Get the camera angle right

Aesthetically speaking, one of the worst angles for a camera is pointed upward at the subject being filmed. However, you're often looking down at your laptop or monitor's camera. Instead, stack your laptop on books or risers for your videos or purchase a separate camera to mount at eye level or just above you. This is a much more flattering and commanding angle (and no one will be able to see up your nose!).

3. Think about your background

You don't necessarily need to place yourself in front of a sprawling bookshelf full of thick legal encyclopedias. However, you may also want to reconsider sitting in front of a blank white wall. Find a good spot in your office, home, or elsewhere that provides an aesthetically pleasing background. If you shoot your videos outdoors, make sure you have a good microphone that filters out all of the background noise!

4. Press "record"

It's that easy! You'll want to have a question or two in mind, but we don't recommend scripting your videos. Videos that are scripted and recited from memory feel robotic and make you look disconnected from your audience. Instead, just imagine that someone has approached you on the street (or maybe one of your golfing buddies asked you a question on the seventh hole). How would you respond in that scenario? Those are the kinds of off-the-cuff answers that make videos better to watch.

5. Edit (or don't)

Don't worry about jump cuts or doing multiple takes. Aim for between 30 seconds and two minutes of footage. After filming, you can upload your video directly to your website or social media. There's no need to edit unless you want to! If you feel like adding graphics, though, then download a free video editor.

How simple or complex your FAQ videos are is up to you. It's also not uncommon for your video setup to evolve over time. After all, it doesn't make sense dumping hundreds or thousands of dollars into a setup if it's not something you're committed to doing long term. In fact, we've seen several attorneys, accountants, and chiropractors evolve their video strategy over time. It's funny to look back at their old videos and see how bare-bones they appear as compared to their most recent release.

If that's the path you take, that's totally okay. What's most important here is that your videos become the catalyst for all of the content you create. Remember the content multiplication formula we shared in chapter 3? It started with a single video, and that's all you have to do now.

Action Item: Film a Video

Take out your smartphone or fire up your webcam and shoot a 2–3 minute video answering a common question you receive. You don't even need to publish this one if you don't want to. The idea is to just get used to the process of filming yourself answering a question.

Remember: Your audience isn't going to see all of the physical or verbal flaws that you'll pick up on when you watch it back. You will be your biggest critic, but the things you are critiquing aren't actually important to the overall effectiveness of your video. The key is the content, not how bad you think you look (because **you definitely aren't as ugly as you think you are!**).

Chapter 8 ~ Podcasting: The Expertise–Boosting Content Medium

When was the last time you asked someone, "Do you watch TV?" Maybe you've never asked that question! These days, we assume everyone has a big screen in their living room. The real question is, "What TV shows do you like?"

We have officially hit that same point in podcasting. In April 2021, Apple Podcasts announced it had more than 1 million shows on its platform. That's crazy! Podcasting is this decade's TV, and if you're not already part of the wave, now is the time to jump in.

2021 was the year of the podcast. So was 2020. And 2019. And 2018. (Also, 2022, 2023, and beyond will be the year of the podcast.)

As of 2021, 41% of Americans listen to podcasts monthly, and the number of overall listeners has grown by 30% over the last 3 years. In fact, more people (80 million) listen to podcasts than those who own Netflix accounts (69 million)!

Podcasting has been hot for so long that if you or your business doesn't have a show, you might think you missed the boat. But that couldn't be further from the truth. If podcasts are still "in," that means people are still listening to them, loving them, and hunting for new ones to try. Your show could be the next big thing.

We've been on the podcast bandwagon for years. We started our first show, *Law Firm Marketing Minute*, in 2018. It's a short podcast that gives marketing advice to lawyers in quick 5–10 minute episodes. In January 2021, we started our second podcast, *Center Stage,* where we interview lawyers and other industry experts on marketing and business development challenges they have mastered or overcome. *(Subscribe to both on your favorite podcast platform today!)*

Several members of our team also have podcasts they host on their personal time. Needless to say, it's become a fun hobby for many of us that has also provided Spotlight Branding with a great marketing and business development tool. Not only do our podcasts give us great content to share on our website and social media, but our *Center Stage* interviews also give our guests free content they can use to show off their expertise!

And while all of us certainly have the ability to sit down and share the knowledge we've gained over the years, the problem is that many business owners feel intimidated with the production aspect of podcasting. What equipment should they buy? Do they have to take a course in audio editing? How on Earth do they even get their show syndicated on platforms like Apple Podcasts and Spotify? The truth is that it isn't as difficult as you might think.

Podcasting Has Never Been Easier

If you've been putting off starting a podcast because you don't know how or think it's too difficult, we have news for you—podcasting is easy! You don't need fancy equipment or deep pockets, either. Websites like BuzzSprout and LibSyn will let you upload your audio and immediately distribute it to outlets like Spotify, Apple Podcasts, and more with just a couple of clicks.

Even more, because every piece of content you put out positions you as the expert in your field, your podcast episodes certainly contribute. You can monologue about cases, interview clients, or talk shop with your associates—it doesn't matter! Simply having the episodes on your website and social media will lend your firm gravitas and impress visitors.

A podcast is also the ultimate networking tool, especially if you do interviews! Offer those coveted slots to your clients as a perk, hand them out to referral partners to build those relationships, or send invitations to the lawyers, potential partners, and celebrities you'd love to meet. You may need to send a lot of invites, but in the end, you'll win the numbers game and fatten your list of connections. (Plus, your guests will feel like they're a big deal because they were invited onto a show!)

Still, we understand how intimidating it can be to dive into a world you're completely unfamiliar with. Luckily for you, we've already gone through the learning curve of getting one (or several) podcasts off the ground. Here are a few things we learned along the way.

1. Just get started

Our CEO, Marc Cerniglia, learned this the hard way. He had the idea for his own podcast, *Zoho My Business,* at least a year before he started the show. When he finally got to work, his show reached 300 followers after just five episodes! Imagine how many more he could have had if he'd started sooner. You can learn from his mistake: Just do it, even if you don't feel ready. Just like your videos, your shows can (and will) improve with time and practice.

2. Factor in your strengths and weaknesses

Your podcast should fit your personal style, habits, and discipline. *Law Firm Marketing Minute* has short episodes because that format plays to our strengths. We're good communicators, so talking for a few minutes is easy! It also factors in our weaknesses: We don't necessarily have the patience to sit down and edit an hour long episode.

3. Pursue your passion

Marc got the idea for *Zoho My Business* when Spotlight Branding switched to the Zoho app suite and discovered he had a passion for the intersection of software and business. Turning that interest into a podcast was (and is) fun! If you focus on your passion, creating content will be easier, more enjoyable, and will resonate with listeners.

4. Be consistent

When Marc started *Zoho My Business*, he was really consistent with the first few episodes. That's how he got 300 followers so quickly! But then, COVID–19 happened and he took a long break. Most of his followers hung around, but he knows he would have had more momentum if he'd kept up the consistency.

5. Ask for help if you need it

If the production aspect is still a little scary, there are several companies out there (including us) who provide podcast production and hosting services. All you have to do is press "record" and send them the audio file. Regardless, don't let your fear of the unknown prevent you from creating a podcast. There are a ton of solutions to help you overcome those fears.

> ### Action Item: Do Some Research
>
> The real reason why so many business owners are hesitant about doing a podcast is a simple fear of the unknown. There are over a million podcasts out there, so it shouldn't be too hard to find some shows by people who work in your particular industry. Subscribe to a few and listen to a handful of episodes. But don't just listen for the subject matter. Listen to the audio quality, the cadence of the host(s), and how each show is structured. You'll likely be surprised to find that these shows aren't as complicated or polished as you expected, which means those same expectations won't apply to your show.

In case you haven't been convinced it's time to start a podcast yet, here are a few more benefits of having a podcast:

- Length isn't an issue. Unlike blog posts or videos, which need to be shorter to cater to our attention spans, podcasting doesn't generally have to adhere to that restriction because…
- There's no time commitment from your audience. When you just have blogs and videos, you're essentially asking your audience to commit their complete attention to reading the entire post or watching the entire video. Podcasting allows people to listen while they commute, work out, mow their lawn, etc.
- It allows you to really show off your knowledge. Because blogs and videos need to be condensed in order to be more easily consumed, you have to cut a lot of information (or create several posts/videos in a series). With a podcast, you can

talk for as long as you want and cover every possible scenario on your given topic without any constraints. (However, we don't recommend 4-hour episodes on anything!)

What You Need to Get Started

The obvious place to start is by getting a good microphone. But investing in one doesn't mean you have to break the bank. We use a Blue Snowball microphone for *The Law Firm Marketing Minute* and *Center Stage*, which costs only about $50. Other good options include the Blue Yeti or the Samson Q2U.

Beyond your microphone, it's all about what other accessories you might need.

- A windscreen or pop filter can smooth out the harsher sounds you make with your Ps, Ts, Ss, and more.
- A boom mic stand can help reposition your microphone to a different place if you don't want it sitting in front of you.
- If you want to record a video version of your podcast, a ring light can balance out the often imperfect lighting in an office (a good webcam might also be beneficial).
- If you're recording an interview, you may want to get a small, 2- or 4-channel mixer to run your microphones through rather than trying to balance two separate audio tracks on your computer.

Planning Your Show

So you have your equipment, now you're ready to go, right? Before you push "Record," you should make sure you answer these questions first:

1. Will you be the host, or will there be multiple?

If you're working in a big firm that covers several areas of expertise and multiple people want to participate, you may want to consider sharing hosting duties for the show depending on the topic being covered.

2. How long will the episodes be?

While you don't need to aim for 3 hour episodes like some of the more popular podcasts out there, you can easily talk for 20, 30, or even 45 minutes. Even just 10 minutes is more than enough for a quality podcast episode.

3. How often will new episodes come out?

Make sure you're consistent. While weekly episodes are the industry standard, it's not uncommon for successful podcasters to publish bi-weekly or even monthly.

4. Will your show be a topic discussion or contain interviews with outside guests?

If your show will just be you monologuing about a topic, great! If you're going to have guests on, make sure you have an ongoing system in place to ensure a steady stream of episodes. If you're unsure of what to cover on your show, we've included some sample prompts below.

Business Law or Financial Pros:

- Tips for how to start, wind down, or sell a business and navigating the taxes/fees along the way
- Interviews with business owners in your area discussing the legal or financial lessons they've learned

Immigration Law:

- Explanations of all of the various immigration visas and policies
- Stories from clients or referral sources about their immigration experience

Family Law:

- Tips on navigating the divorce process from start to finish and any issues along the way
- Tips for life after divorce, both legally and personally

Criminal Law:

- Discussing current or past criminal cases and explaining the legal aspects involved
- Discussion on current laws in your area and how they affect your audience

Chiropractic:
- Health tips
- Explanations of how different subluxations effect different parts of the body

Home Services:
- How–to guide to fix anything (this works well with a video component!)
- Tips for improving your home

Lastly, make sure you have a logo and music beds for your show. A freelance designer can easily take your firm's logo and marry it to a graphic with the title of your show. From there, other freelancers can create custom music beds with radio–quality voiceovers for your intro and outro. The script doesn't have to be complicated, either. Just introduce your show and let people know where they can go to learn more. Here's an example:

Intro: "You're listening to The Law and You, where each week we look at the laws governing our society and explaining how they affect you. Here's your host, Attorney Kevin Jones."

Outro: "Thanks for listening! To learn more, visit kevinjoneslaw.com"

These small projects can be completed on Upwork or Fiverr for less than $100 total.

Recording and Producing Your Podcast

One of the advantages podcasting has over video is that you don't have as much of a battle with your own insecurities. When we watch ourselves on video, it's easy to nitpick and be self-critical over our appearance and mannerisms. Podcasting eliminates that. However, we can still be critical and cringe when we hear ourselves talk. Here are a couple of tips to help you overcome that.

1. Study the "art" of podcasting.

Gary Vaynerchuk says you should study something for up to 50 hours before you participate in it. Chances are you already listen to a couple of different podcasts, but the next time you do, listen as more than just a consumer. Study how the hosts open and close each show. Listen to their cadence and style and see how other people are actually running a show.

2. Prepare, but don't overdo it.

It's best to go into each show with an idea of what points you want to make. While you can launch into a stream of consciousness, you still want to have some idea of where you're going. Conversely, do NOT script your entire show. That's a lot of unnecessary time and your show will sound boring and robotic.

3. Do a couple of test episodes.

It's okay if your first few episodes are imperfect and even clunky. Do a couple of test runs to see how it goes. Take notes on where you can improve, and keep them top-of-mind for when you officially launch.

4. Have fun!

Podcasting is a ton of fun, and we've found that both introverts and extroverts alike really enjoy doing them. There's something that's just really cool about sitting in front of a microphone and showing off your expertise.

When you're ready to start recording, all you have to do is plug your microphone into your computer, open up your recording software, and press "Record." For Mac users, we recommend GarageBand. For PC users, download Audacity. It's a free software that provides a robust set of production tools, most of which you won't need until you ultimately decide to beef up your producer skills.

Once you're recording, just be sure to talk directly into your microphone. You don't need to be pressed up close against it, but you also don't need to be super far away. A good rule of thumb is to be about 12 inches away.

When you're done, all you really need to do is drag and drop your music beds on each end of the recording. Unless you had awkwardly long periods of dead air, a distracting phone that kept going off in the background, or a lot of *uh*'s and *um*'s, you don't need to spend a lot of time actually producing the show.

Remember—no one is actually expecting an NPR–quality broadcast from you. The microphones we recommended earlier in this chapter are already high–quality and better than what you'd create using your computer's built–in microphone, so by default it will already sound amazing. A more natural sounding show will engage your listeners and make them feel like they're right in the room with you and part of your conversation.

Once you have your episode ready, it's on to syndication. Podcast episodes work just like a website—they need to be put on a hosting server. Luckily, services like Libsyn, PodBean, or BuzzSprout make this easy. You just have to upload your episode and (after initially setting up the syndication feeds, which these hosts make super easy to do) these sites handle the rest. For less than $20/month, your episodes will automatically appear on the biggest platforms:

- Apple Podcasts
- Pandora
- Spotify
- Google Podcasts
- iHeart
- Amazon Podcasts
- And more!

Promotion and Metrics

Once your podcast is live, it's all about making sure people know about it and tune in. When it comes to sharing and promoting your podcast, you should definitely do the following:

- *Post the episodes on your website.* Your hosting provider can generate embed codes that you can use to place your podcast episodes directly onto your website. (Remember our content multiplication formula?)
- *Share the episodes on your social media channels.* Post new episode announcements on Facebook, Twitter, LinkedIn, and Google My Business. Some platforms, like BuzzSprout, even allow you to create video clips from your episodes that you can post on Instagram and TikTok!

- *Announce it to your email list.* If you're sending out a regular email newsletter, include a section where you recap your recent episodes (and guests, if applicable).

Remember though, your podcast will NOT be a lead generation tool. It is primarily a referral and business development tool. And while there are readily available metrics based on download numbers for your podcast, unless you already have a well–established brand and a huge audience, those numbers may be small and disappointing at first. But keep these things in mind:

1. With consistent promotion, your downloads will increase over time.

2. Just because you've released a new episode doesn't mean the previous one no longer has value! If your topics are evergreen, you can always recycle them in your marketing content and you can point new leads/prospects to them whenever they enter your marketing ecosystem.

In the end, having your own podcast can provide a ton of great benefits for your firm. The only thing standing in your way is the decision to get started. Everything else is a lot easier than you think.

Chapter 9 ~ Social Media: Your Community Touchpoint Hub

LinkedIn came into the world in 2002, followed by Facebook in 2004, and Twitter in 2006. By now, it's highly likely that you and/or your business have a presence on at least one of those platforms. If you've been posting consistently, great! But chances are that at least one of your profiles has been neglected.

Open a new tab on your browser right now and bring up your firm's social media accounts. Don't just pull up one—open everything you have, including Facebook, Instagram, Tumblr, Alignable, Twitter, etc. Now, look at your most recent post. How long ago was it posted?

Thousands of businesses neglect their social media accounts, and every single one of them is stabbing themselves in the back because of it. You might not feel the wound yet, but trust us, it's there. Your firm is bleeding potential clients.

The first thing people wonder when they pull up a neglected social media account is, "Is this place even open?" In a worst-case scenario, they do a bit of scrolling, decide you've probably closed your doors, and move on. In a best-case scenario, they figure out you're open but still don't call because the neglect makes your business appear disorganized and inattentive.

So how can you bring your social media accounts back to life and turn this weakness into an asset? Creating a schedule and posting consistently is the easiest way! At a minimum, you should create a post every single day. (Reference our content multiplication formula in chapter 3 for an easy way to do that!)

This does mean that sometimes your posts will get repetitive, but repetition isn't a bad thing. One of the concerns we hear most often from our clients is that they fear that repetitive content will be boring or monotonous. If you share those concerns, that's understandable, but the reality is that rather than boring readers, repetitive posts are actually key to getting them engaged! In fact, repetitive content is a proven digital marketing strategy that will help your firm succeed, net you more leads, and keep your practice areas top of mind.

For starters, repetition is the best way to drive home a message and build your brand. Think about the ending of a Nike commercial. It's always the same: Fade to black, then the words "Just Do It" and the signature white swoosh. That's the empowering message Nike wants you to get, and they've drilled it (and their branding) in to everyone's heads with repetition. You can do the same by repeating your blogs, videos, and social media posts to drive home the message of what you do.

The biggest thing, though, is that repetitive posts will help you catch the members of your audience who missed it the first (or second, or third) time. A brilliant journalist once said to his recruits, "It's only after we've written about a problem long enough to be sick of it that readers will finally realize it exists." He recognized that not everyone was reading his newspapers every day and that repeating the message would eventually resonate with the audience.

The same holds true for your social media platforms. Everyone's timeline is controlled by algorithms (some more strict against business pages than others), so the likelihood that every single one of your posts will show up on every audience member's timeline is virtually impossible. To put it differently, no one is browsing your social media feed as often as you. What's old in your eyes will be fresh for them. Additionally, you're also competing with all of the other friends, businesses, and content creators that they like and follow. **It will absolutely take multiple attempts to get in front of everyone.**

The last point we'll make on this is that repetition will actually save you money and time. We've shown you how easy it is to turn one piece of content into more than 50. And while the pieces will be similar, they'll get you maximum impact with minimum input. By repeating your content or variations of it, you will save money and time. For completely unique content, you'd have to pay through the nose to achieve the same results!

How to Be Successful on Social Media

We'll go ahead and warn you right now—this section isn't going to contain the secret formula for going viral, gaining millions of followers, and becoming the next social media star. In fact, if your goal on social media is to go viral, you'll become disenchanted with social media altogether (and likely have a library of cringe-inducing content to go with it). Instead, social media should be used as your platform to provide helpful, evergreen information. You're not selling or promoting, you're just there to help.

Now that we've established the mindset you should have going in, let's talk about the things you need to do in order to get the most out of your social media presence.

1. Establish a presence exclusively for your business

You'd be surprised by just how many small business owners neglect to make separate pages for their business, instead choosing to rely on their personal social media accounts for marketing. We always recommend making separate business accounts, starting with Facebook, Twitter, and LinkedIn. This will help you separate your business life from your personal life and give you a second way to reach people. The primary reason we suggest starting with Facebook, Twitter, and LinkedIn is because you can share the same photos, videos, or text on all three platforms, making it easy to cross-post the same content. (Using a scheduling app like Hootsuite makes it easy to post to all three platforms at once!)

Once you've established a rhythm there, you can add other networks like Instagram, Google My Business, TikTok, and more.

2. Create a sharing formula

Use our content multiplication formula as a reference tool. You don't have to do it exactly the way we laid it out, but make sure to set benchmarks for each week. Nail down numbers for each objective so you can just "plug and play" to stay consistent. Remember—you can share the same post multiple times on different platforms or with different captions. Aim for a content balance with a mix of media types, and don't forget to throw some fun posts, like inspirational quotes, in the mix for interest.

Once you start consistently executing this formula, you can spend a couple of dollars to boost the posts you make on Facebook and LinkedIn. This allows you to bypass those restrictive algorithms and lets more people see your content. That exposure is definitely worth the price.

3. Don't try to be an influencer

When it comes to social media, 99% of users—businesses or otherwise—try to play an engagement game. They think likes, comments, and shares are currency and that they can only win on social media by chasing them. While this might be true for celebrities, food bloggers, and billion-dollar companies like Nike, in our experience, lawyers, accountants, and other professional industries won't convert social media leads by aiming for engagements. The best thing for you to do is to abandon the social media "influencer" dream and reach for a new archetype: social media resource.

Think about it this way: Do you think a guy looking for a divorce is going to like a divorce lawyer's post? What about a woman facing bankruptcy? Is she going to share her secret with all of her friends? Of course not. White-collar businesses typically solve problems, and often these problems are personal, embarrassing, and unsharable. This makes becoming an influencer nearly impossible, and you'll waste your time trying.

Additionally, the most eye-catching posts that go viral aren't exactly informative. This isn't an absolute rule, but in general, social media posts that grab the eye and generate engagements aren't the most informative ones out there. Most posts that get likes on social media are pretty, sexy, or shocking. None of those things will help bring you clients that are educated, informed, and ready to work with you.

Lastly, you don't want your potential clients to see you as an attention-grabber or an alarmist—you want them to trust you and view you as competent, confident, and experienced. If you're constantly pedaling irrelevant stories or begging for likes, you'll build wariness, not trust.

So, what should a smart business owner do? The businesses we've seen succeed on social media are the ones who use it as a tool to educate their audiences, reinforce their expertise, and stay top of mind. By filling their feeds with relevant, well-researched, expert content, they build trust with their followers, convert them to clients, and inspire referrals.

Action Item: Create Your Social Media Schedule

Don't worry about writing up all of your posts just yet. Instead, figure out *what* you're going to post. If you use our content multiplication formula, you have plenty of options. Look at the sample below and create a similar, repeatable schedule for your business.

Week 1

Monday: A blog post or a video

Tuesday: A link to your free download

Wednesday: A blog post or a video

Thursday: A 3rd party article relevant to your business

Friday: A motivational quote or graphic

Week 2

Monday: A 3rd party article relevant to your business

Tuesday: A link to your e–newsletter signup

Wednesday: A blog post or a video

Thursday: A call–to–action with info about your business

Friday: A motivational quote or graphic

Chapter 10 ~ Email: Your Most Valuable Marketing Asset

When we pitch email newsletters to our clients, we're often met with the verbal equivalent of an eye roll. You know the arguments: "Nobody wants another email in their inbox," "No one is going to read my email newsletter," and "I hate getting email newsletters—when I do, I put them in the trash or mark them as spam, and my audience is going to do that, too!"

That attitude is unfortunate because we know for a fact that when our clients send out an email each month, they inevitably generate more referrals. Why? Because none of us have enough time to personally stay in touch with everyone on our contact list. Sure, you might make space in your schedule to meet with key referral sources or colleagues, but there's no way you can stay in touch with everyone you've met in the last 15 years. Now, imagine you could maintain those relationships. How is it possible they wouldn't lead to at least a few more referrals?

Email isn't the only way to stay in touch with your contacts, but it's the first step. Even if only 20% of the people you send to open your email, you'll be reaching many more than you could have if you had tried to do it on an individual basis. And don't forget, even the people who don't open your newsletter still see it, keeping your firm's name top of mind. We've had leads call us who have gotten our email newsletter for years and rarely opened it. Still, when it's time to do business, they call. (Also, remember the airplane story from chapter 3? That was made possible by email.)

But before you dive headfirst into your email campaigns, heed this warning: **Do NOT get caught up in analytics.**

The email marketing landscape is shifting. Privacy laws are becoming more restrictive when it comes to the data that marketers can collect from their email recipients. For years, marketing companies judged an email's success on open and click–through rates. Even then, those analytics never told the whole story, and now, they're going to tell even less.

And while knowing your open rate and click–through rates can be helpful, the #1 benefit of an email marketing campaign isn't the data it gives you. It's the valuable content that it provides to your email list.

This content educates your readers, positions you as the expert, and keeps your firm top of mind. Ideally the people on your list will open your emails to get the full impact of that content, but the truth is that open rates matter less than you think. Your email marketing will still make a significant impact and bring you referrals and repeat business even if no one ever opens those emails.

Just seeing your firm's name and a subject line related to what you do is enough to build your brand, remind people of what you do, and make a referral or repeat business more likely. Plus, everyone has email! And they're probably more willing to hand over their email address than their phone number. This makes email just as valuable as text message marketing, and you'll get better results if you use both.

To put it succinctly, there are three reasons to keep emailing your clients, prospects, and referral partners even if email analytics go to the dogs:

1. Content matters more than open rates.
2. Even unopened emails make an impact.
3. Email is a reliable, universal way to stay in touch.

Email may not be sexy or exciting, but it's a tried-and-true marketing strategy that's not going anywhere, and if it's working for you today it will still work just as well regardless of what new privacy laws become enacted.

How to Create a Profitable Newsletter

Sending out an email newsletter is one of the best ways to stay in touch with your network, build your brand, bring in leads, and generate referrals. This is common knowledge among small business owners, but many of them still don't hit the send button—why?

Well, if you've never put together a newsletter, the prospect of spending time and effort to create one might be intimidating. However, the process is much easier than you think, especially when it's in digital form. In less than an hour, you can create a DIY email newsletter that will take you only minutes to maintain each month.

1. Sign up for a platform

There are plenty of email newsletter platforms to choose from, and you can create an account for little to no cost. We use MailChimp, but Constant Contact and AWeber are great options, too.

2. Choose a template

Don't waste your time building a newsletter from scratch or getting something custom coded (that may still not render properly in an inbox). If you're going to do that, hire a professional company to design and program it for you. Rather, just about every email marketing platform offers newsletter templates, complete with visual editors. All you have to do is customize the colors, add your logo, and fill in the content.

3. Drag and drop your existing content

You don't have to reinvent the wheel: Simply pop in the blog posts and videos you've already made, and rotate them each month (remember our content multiplication formula!). You can even add a section for announcements and specials. If you don't have content available, consider this your reminder to create some.

4. Create and maintain an email list

You need to add the email addresses of your past and current clients, referral partners, and other contacts to your chosen platform. If you're lucky, your office CRM will give you the option to export your addresses and integrate them automatically. If not, this step might take some time, but it will be worth it! After the initial input, make a system to add new addresses each month.

5. Send the newsletter monthly

You don't need to send it daily or weekly. A single monthly email has proven to work wonders for our clients, and we've heard from several that they receive multiple requests for new business with each email that goes out.

As you're going through this process, remember that your newsletter doesn't have to be perfect. Something is better than nothing, and you can improve it over time.

Final Tips for Successful Emails

While sending emails is valuable, your email list is actually your most valuable marketing asset. Your business is nothing without it. The files upon files of customer data that you have stashed away in your email can give you more insight and direction than most metrics, yet many business leaders know very little about their list, much less how to utilize it.

A great list has a few components. It's usually more than just an Excel spreadsheet with names, physical addresses, email addresses, preferences, and phone numbers. But if you don't even have that, then you need to do some serious updating before you go any further!

Start by scrubbing your list. Remove any names that are no longer prudent. Then, call the remaining people on the list and verify contact information or ask for additional details. Make this an impossible offer to turn down by providing a reward or something of value to those who opt to share more details with you (the offer of free legal/financial/health information delivered to them each month is more than enough). As more people offer their information, you'll have multiple tools to market directly to them.

Once you have a brand new, scrubbed, beautiful list, it's time to break it down. Your list can be segmented into multiple components to provide a scope of your business's well–being and to pinpoint target areas (and your email platform like MailChimp or Constant Contact can help you do this). Start with three "buckets":

1. Prospects
2. Customers
3. Bad Leads

From there, you can break the list down even further to include:

- Canceled customers
- Hot leads
- Customers with high spending habits
- New sales
- And anything else relevant to your business

As you categorize your list into various buckets, a plan will emerge. Your team can develop campaigns to upsell clients who may need more of the services or products you offer while pinpointing those who could be resold on your company. This segmented data is then a powerful tool to help you specifically target your lists rather than casting a wide net and only catching a few leads.

One of the easiest ways to target each group is through relationship marketing. Increase your content production, and **keep hitting your customers with your message**, using the information from your list to guide you. Once you have your monthly newsletter in place, you can start to send a few physical postcards. Next, host a Facebook Live event with that very same information and invite a specialty group of people from your list (i.e., your hot leads or loyal customers).

Each time you curate a message specifically for a segmented population, you are creating a message that will land right where they need it the most. But don't let off the gas. Most readers only remember about 10% of what they consume, so keep communicating!

With a targeted list, you should have no problem finding a new tactic, a new device, or a new platform to get your message out to the people who need to hear it most. It all starts with perfecting—and updating!—your list.

Beyond that, keep these final points in mind with your emails:

1. Make sure your subject line is the title of your featured blog or video.

In other words, don't make "Smith Law Firm Newsletter" the subject line because you can't expect your entire list to always remember what area of law Smith Law Firm practices. Instead, if your subject line is your featured content, (i.e., "5 Tips for Co–parenting During the Holidays"), then people will more easily associate the subject line with how you can help.

2. Keep the content specific to your business.

Don't throw in recipes unless you're in the food industry. Don't include irrelevant articles that have nothing to do with your business.

3. Make sure you're constantly adding new emails to your contact list.

Anytime you network, receive an intake form, or have someone contact you online, add their email to your contact list.

Chapter 11 ~ Understanding Your Marketing Success

Congratulations! You now have your playbook. However, any good coach will tell you that a playbook is worthless unless you have a good team in place to execute those plays. The nice thing about marketing is that, even if you're just a solo operation, there are resources out there you can take advantage of (yes, we're talking about marketing vendors like us).

You can also handle your marketing yourself, just don't sacrifice too many billable hours or precious nights and weekends doing it. If you have an in–house marketing team, make sure you have a strategy in place so they can flawlessly execute everything you need them to.

Regardless of whether or not you delegate these important tasks, you as a business owner still have a role to play in determining your marketing's success. For starters, (and we're sure you're already aware of this), marketing is expensive. Buying pay–per–click advertising, hiring a copywriter to create compelling content, sending out print mailers—all these things cost money. That said, in our experience, the cost of marketing isn't what frustrates most business owners. What they hate is worrying that they are spending thousands of dollars on the wrong marketing.

It's an understandable concern, but really, you only need to do one thing to ensure you're not pouring your marketing budget down the drain: Measure your own success.

When you employ a third–party vendor like us to do your marketing, it can be tempting to "set it and forget it." In other words, you might feel compelled to leave it up to the vendor to keep track of your ROI. **Don't give in to that temptation!** No one has a better understanding of your goals and the full scope of your firm's marketing efforts than you. If you're ready to take charge of your own marketing destiny and stop wasting your money, take these three steps today.

STEP 1: Understand what matters

Not all data points are created equal. Despite what some marketers will tell you, an increase in Twitter followers doesn't directly translate to more revenue. The first step to measuring your marketing success is deciding what's worth measuring. Focus on statistics that move the needle like the number of referrals, new clients, and returning clients that your efforts generate.

STEP 2: Define success

What does the word "success" mean to you? Consider what your goals are and what achieving them would look like. Do you need to get a certain number of referrals or new clients per month to feel like your marketing is working? Figure out what matters to you, then communicate your goals to your vendor.

STEP 3: Accept responsibility

Whether you're a business owner, marketing manager, or project lead, you need to accept responsibility for tracking your marketing success. Start making spreadsheets—then use them! This doesn't mean you have to do all of the marketing yourself, but tracking your own results is empowering and gives your firm independence, letting you see for yourself whether your investments are paying off.

Action Item: Identify Your Key Metrics

It's time to let go of those vanity metrics, at least when it comes to determining the overall success/failure of your marketing. (You can still keep them as FYI numbers). Instead, look at the data points that truly determine whether or not your business is growing. Here are some ideas, but whatever you choose, make sure you hold yourself accountable for ensuring any marketing or other business development you do contributes to the metrics that drive your business forward.

- Referrals
- Average case/client/product value
- Conversion/win rate
- Churn/retention
- New clients
- Revenue (one–time or recurring) gained/lost

So how exactly do you measure your success? Well, imagine that it's a Monday morning. You walk into your office and your secretary says, "I have good news!" Which of these two things would you want to hear next?

1. "We gained 10,000 new followers on Instagram!"
2. "We got referrals from three clients, and I just booked them all for consultations!"

#2, right? You probably picked that one because consultations are almost guaranteed to make you money, while Instagram followers don't put anything directly into your pocket. And you're absolutely right. Not all good news is created equal—and neither are all metrics.

When it comes to marketing, many small business owners and marketing companies don't understand the difference between helpful metrics and useless ones, which we like to call "vanity numbers." If you're focused on tracking data like email open rates, Facebook likes, or Instagram followers, then you're getting stuck in vanity land. And if the marketing company you've hired is doing that, then they're doing you a disservice! The truth is that most people don't make money just because of their clicks, their views, or their engagements.

Instead of focusing on vanity numbers, you should prioritize tracking revenue–generating results like new clients, referrals, and average case/customer value. Once you figure out what those metrics are, you can create spreadsheets or hire a marketing company that sees eye to eye with you on which metrics are important. Marketing companies should want to help you grow your business instead of just wowing you with statistics.

Finally—and this is the hardest part—if you have an outside marketing team, you'll need to collaborate with them. Only you really know how many referrals and new clients you're getting, or what your average case value is. By communicating that with them, they can see what's working and what isn't and double down on helping you succeed.

This playbook will help you succeed in this arena because your content marketing strategy will not only help you increase referrals by helping you stay top of mind, but it will also help the rest of your marketing efforts work better. And even though marketing can get expensive, not all marketing has to incur a cost. Networking is a marketing activity. Speaking is a marketing activity. Holding workshops is a marketing activity. And they're all free.

The point is that your website, your videos, your blogs, your newsletters, your podcast, whatever you have—that content is actually all going to enhance your existing marketing and networking efforts and activities. So you have to understand that the more you do in that arena, the further your content is going to go.

Additionally, are you able to charge the rates that you want? When you are putting out an effective content strategy, you are building up yourself and your firm as the experts and you're often able to command the rates that you want and deserve. When you have that in place, you'll start to see a better conversion on your existing marketing efforts.

Ready to put it all in place and realize the marketing success you've been dreaming of? It's time to go!

Chapter 12 ~ The Obligatory SEO Chapter

We suppose no digital marketing book would be complete without something devoted to search engine optimization (SEO). After all, you've likely been pitched SEO services your entire business career and likely think it's as ubiquitous a marketing strategy as Band–Aid is to adhesive bandages. But it's not.

We spent quite a bit of time on why SEO sucks in our previous book, *The Ultimate Solo Lawyer's Guide to More Referrals and Better Clients*, but we'll wrap up this book with a little reminder as to why this shouldn't be something you build your entire marketing strategy around.

In July 2021, Google's algorithm team destroyed the marketing strategies of hundreds of small businesses with just a few clicks. The updates Google made constituted just another day at the office for them (after all, Google updates its algorithms hundreds, sometimes thousands of times every year). But for many small business owners, those clicks were disastrous! Overnight, their companies disappeared from Google's front page and were buried deep in the search results—exactly where they had paid thousands of dollars not to be.

What happened? Well, those unlucky businesses bet on the SEO game and lost. Lawyers, accountants, home services, chiropractors, etc. often pour a huge share of their marketing dollars into SEO rankings, paying SEO companies to get them to the top. But what they usually don't consider is that **Google doesn't profit from SEO**. They don't care who ranks high and who ranks low. They just care that people are using Google.

If you play the SEO game, Google's team has the potential to screw you over with every algorithm update. It will be Russian roulette every time whether the change is in your favor. You'll never know when it's coming and neither will your SEO provider. If you asked Google, we imagine they'd simply say, "It's not personal, it's just business."

This Google insanity is just one reason why you shouldn't rely on SEO marketing. It usually hurts businesses more than it helps them—and here are three more reasons why.

1. Your odds of winning are almost nonexistent

Think about how many businesses there are in your geographic area who do the same thing you do. Can you beat out all of them—on a purely financial basis—for one of the 10 spots on Google's first page of search results?

You might have a chance against similar businesses of your size, but big law, national firms, or franchises will eat your marketing budget for lunch. It makes no sense to try to compete with them, especially because SEO leads are generally only price shopping in the first place. They will leave you at the drop of a hat when something cheaper comes along.

2. SEO creates a terrible user experience

If you cater your online content to the algorithm overlords, you'll alienate another group of people: your potential clients. Blogs stuffed with keywords and backlinks that rehash current news stories don't make for very good reading. At best, leads will discount your blog posts. At worst, they might think you're a robot that doesn't know much about your industry or can't write coherently.

3. Content succeeds where SEO fails

There's no reason to pay through the nose for SEO when there's a much better, more cost-effective, more reliable option out there: content marketing. Content that caters to people, not algorithms, will position you as the expert, remind readers of what you do, and keep your firm top of mind. And it's a safe bet!

The truth is that you do not need SEO to run a successful business, but **most marketing companies won't tell you that.** Yes, catering to SEO will raise your Google rankings. However, unless you're engaged in an aggressive, all-out SEO effort, the boost you get will likely only take you from Page 10 of the search results to Page 5—which is really no difference at all. (Keep in mind that regardless of whether you make any SEO effort, as long as you have a website, people actually looking for your firm will find you on Google just fine.)

In our experience, you're better off letting go of SEO completely than playing the game halfway. With that in mind, we recommend to our clients that unless they're prepared to go all-in, they're better off reallocating the money and time they're spending on SEO to other things. We also don't talk about or label anything we do as SEO with our clients because 99.9% of the time, it's a losing proposition. That's why we focus on content, not algorithms—and it works.

As if this book hasn't shown you a variety of marketing strategies that are more important than SEO, let's run through a quick summary of five things that you should be focused on first.

1. Developing a clearly defined brand

Why did you become a business owner in the first place? Did you open your own business because of your entrepreneurial spirit, to make a ton of money, or to help people in need? What do you do differently that sets you apart from the other people in your city that also do what you do?

How effectively you brand yourself goes a long way toward determining the success of your firm. Being just "another lawyer" or "another chiropractor" or "another CPA" in your city isn't going to work. The internet allows customers to conduct more research on their options than ever before. You need to brand yourself as THE expert in your city and stand out from the crowd. You need to make yourself so memorable and attractive to your target clients that they view you as the ONLY choice to get the job done.

2. Having a website that highlights and reinforces your credibility

Does your website reflect your expertise and make you look like the credible professional that you are? A website is like the digital version of your physical office. You're probably not working out of a derelict shack, so why would you allow your website to be the digital equivalent?

If you're spending the majority of your marketing budget on SEO and your website looks terrible, you could actually be doing more harm than good. Sure, being on the first page of a Google search is nice, but if hundreds of people are arriving at a bad website, they're likely to go somewhere else and you've lost out on their business.

What does a great website look like? It's more than having sleek images and colors that pop. It's about the information you're placing on the site. Do customers get a good sense of who you are? Can they see your face and mannerisms through photos and videos? Are you displaying your knowledge and expertise by creating blog content? Are you providing educational resources? Your website needs to be more than just your name and contact information. It needs to be a knowledge center. This is how you position yourself as an expert.

3. Forming a solid networking strategy

The internet is great, but it's not a magical place that sends eager clients to your door. You still have to get out there and build relationships in your community. Referrals are the best way to grow your business, and your internet marketing presence should support your networking and referral strategy.

What does your strategy look like? Are you active in local business groups like BNI, Rotary, or the Chamber of Commerce? Look for speaking engagements, too. Speaking at an event is a good way to get your name out there and connect with people who may need your services in the future. If there's nothing in your area, start your own monthly event to bring people together.

4. Attracting the right clients

SEO can drive additional traffic to your site, but unless it's done by someone who knows what they're doing, you will likely get a lot of irrelevant traffic to your website. We've seen SEO tactics that would bring in traffic from the other side of the country from people who aren't even relevant to our client's practice area. If the goal is to increase website traffic, then SEO has done its job. But if your goal is to get qualified prospects through your door, SEO alone won't get the job done.

While the higher number of website visitors looks impressive, the results are meaningless unless they translate to new clients (remember what we said about vanity metrics?). Alternatively, by building referrals and having an online presence that brands you as the expert in your community, you'll attract the right kinds of people that you want to do business with. And if you have a great website, they'll be more informed and ready to do business with you.

5. Implementing an unforgettable follow–up system

People are busy. If you're not following up and checking in on past clients or referral sources, chances are they're going to forget about you and what you do. Having a system in place where you can remind people of what you do and how you can help them not only provides an extra touch of customer service, but it contributes to the growth of your business. The best part—this book has given you all of the tools you need to make that happen!

SEO isn't the answer to your online presence. It's overrated and overemphasized. These other things are more important, and our clients have experienced dramatic growth following this path (and you can too!). Don't lose focus on these goals!

A Final Word on Pay–per–Click

Many businesses spend thousands of dollars on pay–per–click advertising every year to get their firms noticed. Competition is stiff! If you're a pay–per–click convert, you're probably always on the hunt for strategies that will increase your conversion rate and boost your ad performance. One of those strategies is so simple it's often ignored: content marketing (you're not surprised we said that, right?). We've said it before and we'll say it again: High-quality content makes all of your firm's marketing work better! This includes pay-per-click ads. Here are two ways to make it happen.

1. Pack your home page/landing page

Your pay-per-click ads should direct leads to your website or an offer-specific landing page. Once they get there, you can strategically use content to convince them to stay and convert. Embedded FAQ videos are ideal for this, as are testimonials, podcast snippets, and even blogs. Just be careful not to use too many links that will take visitors off your landing page. You want them to stay, not go!

2. Add a secondary conversion tool

If you're running a Google Ads campaign, you probably want leads to ultimately schedule a consultation or fill out a contact form. We call this full-speed-ahead strategy "going for the jugular." It's a great thing to aim for, but if you go for the jugular exclusively, you'll miss out on warm leads that aren't ready to convert. To capture those people, add a secondary conversion tool to your home or landing page. Offer visitors the option to sign up for your print or email newsletter, or give them a free resource (e.g., an exclusive PDF, podcast, or video) in exchange for an email address. That way, they don't have to get all the way in bed with you, but you'll still bring them into your firm's Content Loop and closer to conversion.

However (and we think this book has proven this to be true), you don't need to rely on paid ads or SEO to have a successful marketing strategy. So many business owners have been brainwashed into thinking they should be depending on Google to grow and maintain their business. They've been led to believe that search engines are the only way to generate leads and new business.

Maybe you are that business owner. Maybe you picked up this book because you were frustrated with the results you were getting there. Use this as your sign to make a change.

You don't even have to abandon your paid ads and SEO (because we know that letting go is hard to do). But swap out your old foundation with one centered on quality information and consistent content. It WILL help your business grow. We've seen it happen with hundreds of businesses all over the country.

You just have to take the first step. The playbook is in your hands. Now it's time to turn your business into a winner.

Thank you so much for checking out our content marketing playbook. If you have any questions about the contents of this book, your business's marketing strategy, or anything else, please feel free to reach out to us at Solutions@SpotlightBranding.com or giving us a call at (800) 406-7229.

Spotlight Branding provides all of the marketing services mentioned in this playbook, and we would welcome the opportunity to work with you to help your business meet and exceed its growth goals. Contact us today to learn about our service packages.

www.ingramcontent.com/pod-product-compliance
Lightning Source LLC
Chambersburg PA
CBHW020544220526
45463CB00006B/2184